REPORT ON THE AMERICAN COMMUNIST

MORRIS L. ERNST
AND
DAVID LOTH

REPORT

ON THE

AMERICAN   E 70

COMMUNIST

CAPRICORN BOOKS
NEW YORK

324.27375
E71

CONTENTS

REPORT ON THE AMERICAN COMMUNIST

~~~~~~~~~~~~~~~~~~~~~~~~~~~~~~~~~~~~

CHAPTER ONE

INSIDE THE COMMUNIST

WHEN an American joins the Communist party, he cuts himself off from the rest of the community. He becomes an enemy to the rest of us, and most of us are very much afraid of him. We are afraid because we really know almost nothing about him, what got him into the party, what influences shaped him so that he was party material, what makes him tick.

The thesis of this book is that the people of the United States cannot wisely and successfully combat communism in this country unless they understand Communists. Understanding also will remove fear. So we propose to examine, with the assistance of personal accounts of several hundred men and women who have been in and out of the Communist party, just why they joined and why they left. If we know these facts we will be in a better position to prevent the rank and file, which is the backbone of any party, from joining in the first place. Certainly we would be able to get them out before they have become dangerous agents of a foreign power.

In all the years of anti-Communist activity in this country, no nation-wide effort at such understanding has been made. A few highly articulate ex-members, a few former leaders, have bared themselves with much publicity and excitement. Are they really representative of the membership generally? We want to find out.

In 109 thick volumes of Congressional testimony studied in preparation for this book, we could find virtually nothing elicited except by accident or inadvertence to establish the fundamental facts about the types of people who join the party, their family backgrounds, why they leave, the amount and kind of education they had received.

In seeking to understand the rank and file of party members nearly 300 former Communists have helped us by telling their own experiences, motives, and beliefs. We asked these ex-members and ourselves a number of questions. We give them here, along with a brief summary of some of the answers we found. The evidence for those answers will be found in the chapters that follow.

What is the age at which Americans are most likely to join the Communist party?

The peak age appears to be 18 to 23. In fact a majority of the rank and file have not only joined but have left the party by the time they are 23. The late teens seem to be an especially susceptible time. We have come across quite a few cases of children who became members of the Young Communist League at 14 or so, and left when they grew up—say at 18 or 20. One of the men we interviewed, who left the party at the time of the Stalin-Hitler pact, was then 40 years old—older than most at the time of departure. He recalls exposing his intentions, before they were solidly formed, to a close friend, also a party member, who was 60 years old. The older man also had expressed his doubts about the pact between Stalin and Hitler, but could not nerve himself to act on them. However, to his younger friend he said: "Get out now or you will never get out."

Do members come from working-class homes, middle-class homes, professional backgrounds, business backgrounds, or what?

They have been brought up, in general, in comfort and often in luxury. They are the children of professional men or more than usually successful businessmen, bankers, and ministers. In fact, the Communist party in America seems to be such a highly educated, nonmanual laboring group that at times there would be more rejoicing in its headquarters over the recruiting of one common laborer than over ten Ph.D.'s.

Another factor in the family background that struck us was the extremely high incidence of suicides, desertions, and divorces among the parents, brothers, and sisters, or other close relatives of Communists. This is true not only among those who have written out their stories for us but also among the more widely publicized former members of the party who have played leading roles in investigations and trials.

Equally impressive was the great number of men who had grown up with a marked hostility to an aggressive father who usually was a conservative in politics, and the number of women who thought themselves less than beautiful and complained about an overwhelming mother.

What is the educational level?

The average Communist has had far more schooling than the general population of the country, and the proportion of party members who have been to college is very high. Even more striking is the great number of graduate degrees among them.

What kind of jobs do they hold?

Most of the Communists occupy positions which do not call for any work with their hands. They seem to be found more often in the professions which are entirely intellectual or in jobs which call for no manual dexterity. In the medical profession, they are more likely to be diagnosticians and psychiatrists than surgeons. They tend more toward the law or teaching than to engineering or architecture. They hold clerical jobs in industry rather than work at machines. Even when the party assigns them to work in a given industry, they gravitate toward nonmanual jobs. They seek out jobs as union organizers and officers not only for the influence it will give them but because they are more at home in them than they would be in tending a machine.

Do they join the party for gain, for power, for an ideal, for treachery, for emotional satisfaction, or what?

Seldom is there a single, powerful motive for membership. The Communist, like most of the rest of us, is molded by a complex tissue of motives. Usually he thinks of himself as an idealist joining the party because of his hatred of war, poverty, and discrimination or other injustice. Certainly that is a powerful reason. But millions of others share the hate without becoming Communists. The party members seem to have found in communism an emotional satisfaction which held them—while they remained believing members—even more strongly than their desire to work for peace or reform. An understanding of the psychological factors which lead to that emotional satisfaction is one of the chief aims of this book.

Financial gain is almost never a factor; nearly every former Communist we encountered could and did earn more money out of the party than in it. Power is only a slightly stronger motive. A few of the rank and file manifest a latent desire for power which they think might be fulfilled in a movement which is seeking world power. Treachery is beside the point at the time of joining, for that comes only later and often not at all.

One other influence should be mentioned. In many recruits to communism is an obvious sense of never having "belonged" until they discovered the intense and all-consuming life within the party. These are the men and women who as boys and girls were unpopular or ignored either because of looks or a social stigma or shyness or overeagerness or some other reason which is overlooked in the party.

Some things which have often been supposed to lead the young to communism seem to have little or no effect. These are bad company, poverty, and Communist literature or speakers.

Most Communists seem to have been singularly free from what is generally considered bad company. In fact, in their cases this factor can be allowed only if we consider that parents are bad company. Surprisingly often—at least to us—the Communists as children seem to have been little ladies and gentlemen. They consorted more frequently than the average of their fellows with teachers and ministers and other kids who went to Sunday school. They were found more often in the library or the debating society than in the alley or on the baseball field. They preferred books to magazines.

In our studies, the only influence of poverty in making Communists was during the depression of the early thirties and in the case of a few of the "newly poor." These were the only instances where bitterness over lack of means seemed to play any part at all. So far as can be determined, Communists are seldom recruited from the ranks of the very poor in this country, however it might be in Italy or France or Spain. They suffer from another kind of poverty, a certain poverty of spirit, but are not driven by hunger and cold into the party. Insofar as money is a factor it would appear usually in cases of the newly rich or the children of the wealthy.

Very few of our collaborators mentioned joining the party after reading some particular book or hearing some particular speaker. But apparently in each such case, the real groundwork already had been laid. The book or the orator can be credited with no more than a peg on which the former Communist hangs his memory of the date of his conversion to the party principles. Reading and listening to speeches seem to be as impotent in this realm as in the realm of sex. The printed word has been credited with much power in corrupting youth, whether it be to make a Communist or a pervert, only because the people who give the credit do not care to look at the truth. If this were not the case, those who read obscenity for the vice societies would be uncontrollable sex maniacs by now.

Even the most simple know that books are no substitute for a sex experience. Even the most eloquent orators have won converts only among those who were ready to be converted. We want to learn why some people are ready to be converted to communism.

Are certain personality traits common to all or most Communists?

Although not psychologists, we think that certain generalizations are possible, especially if it is kept in mind that there are exceptions to all of them. (The subject calls urgently for a great deal more study by people who are experts.) In general, then, the stories we have collected suggest these facts:

The psychological quirk which led these several hundred Americans and others they told us about to join the Communist party stems from one or more of these factors: There is a sense of personal inadequacy, whether that in turn was induced by resentment to an overpowering personality in youth, by a specific handicap of a physical or spiritual nature, by some strong frustration, or by an inability to reach independent decisions. A lack of both humor and optimism seems always to have been one of their early characteristics, not greatly affected by experiences during party membership or later. Intellectual preoccupations predominate rather than athletics, for example. (Some of course were good at sports; Paul Robeson was an outstanding athlete, but in general they prefer the debating team or the school paper.) A sense of selfless dedication rather than pushing opportunism is evident in most of them.

This last is so strong that they excuse their alliance with an alien power, Russia, by picturing it as a sacrifice to the cause which will benefit all mankind. Even those who were guilty of actual espionage on behalf of Russia were not bought. They did not spy for money but because they accepted the dogma that Russia is to save the world and any means to that end are justifiable.

While in the party, most although not all members enjoyed the secrecy, the spying on each other which is standard procedure in every Communist cell, the stealth with which the party approaches its objectives. On this score many show no real change of heart even after they leave; they explain and defend such underhanded activity as necessary. Often these are submissive people who want to be told what to do and what to think. They certainly do not want to be leaders. They are happy when someone else assumes the authority to tell them where to work, whether or not they may get married or divorced, what sort of a physician they may consult, the school their children should attend. In fact they had sought the "good mother" when joining the party and when disillusioned declare that the "good mother" has turned into a "bad mother." We have a hunch that the frequent expression of chagrin at having been naïve stems from surprise and pain which derive from the disillusionment felt because of having been "bamboozled" with respect to the selection of "mother Russia" as the good mother.

Is communism more attractive to urban than rural people? To men or women? To the timid or adventurous?

The bulk of the membership is in the big cities, partly because the organizers have been people who believed the best recruits were obtainable in industry or the professions, and partly because the party made its main drive in areas of concentrated population. But it seems to be true, too, that the personality likely to be attracted to communism is also likely to leave the farm for the city. The rural dweller needs to be more skillful with his hands; when he has little manual dexterity, he is likely to move to town. The party's attraction seems to be about equal for men and women. Or rather they often attract each other. Many, especially women, have joined the party after falling in love with a Communist and left it after falling in love with somebody else or losing the beloved. There seems to be a very large group of Communists who have grown up under the aegis of a dominating father or an overpowering mother. This same psychological pattern is revealed in the writings of the more widely publicized former Communists. The rank-and-file party member seems to us to be rather timid than adventurous in thought and ideas, although he can be bold on order, and rather adventurous than timid in personal action. The timidity often approaching complete submissiveness is seen in his conformity to the party line; the adventurousness is displayed in the readiness with which members will uproot themselves from home and job to venture into a new place and new work at the demand of a party boss.

What is the nationality or citizenship of members at different levels of command?

The rank and file is almost entirely native-born. Incidentally, it is almost entirely white, too. The leadership has a great many more foreign-born individuals, and the top command in reality if not in form is Russian.

There are several popular stereotypes of the Communist. One is a foreigner, preferably Russian and bearded, with an inbred hatred of American institutions and concealing a bomb. One is an immigrant who has not been well assimilated and fails to understand his new country. One is a victim of poverty or discrimination or both who is driven by economic despair to accept an alien philosophy. One is a psychopathic traitor, a composite figure drawn from the more lurid witnesses in spy trials and the investigations conducted by right-wing anti-Communists with social pink eye. One is a long-haired intellectual who lives in a world of books and talk but never did an honest day's work with his hands.

None of these fits the actual rank and file, but the last comes closest to hitting the mark. The party boasts more horn-rimmed glasses than beards, more uncalloused palms than foreign accents.

Do professional Communists, the hard core of
the movement, resemble or differ from the rank
and file?

There is a wide gulf between them, although part of the hard core may be recruited, after most careful screening, from the rank and file. The professional is both more cynical and more determined, more supple and more ruthless. The rank and file are far more mixed in their motives. The rank and file accept the Communist doctrine that the cause of communism justifies any means that may further it, but in practice they apply it timidly or shrink from it. The leaders act upon it without scruple. The rank and file are ready to sacrifice themselves for their beliefs. The hard core will sacrifice themselves or anyone else.

What is the religion of party members except
as communism itself has been considered a
religion?

Although a great many of the rank and file were brought
up in church-going families, most of them seem to have
been indifferent or even hostile to the faith of their families
before ever they embraced communism. In general they
remain indifferent after they leave the party. However,
a small minority were ardently pious before entering the
party, and a slightly larger number seem to find solace
in religion after they leave it.

Was the party strengthened or weakened by the
Hoover regime? The Roosevelt New Deal? The
depression? The war? The postwar struggle
with Russia?

By and large the political complexion of government
does not seem to have much influence upon the size of the
party's membership, nor the fervor with which its principles are embraced. The depression did bring it some
recruits but not as many as might have been expected.
The Loyalist fight against Franco in Spain helped the party
here up to at least the time of the attack of Russia on Finland, and our wartime alliance with Russia and admiration
for the heroism of the Russian people as displayed in such
examples as the siege of Leningrad brought the party to its
peak of membership and probably of influence. After the
war, disillusionment with Soviet aims and practices caused

a clear loss. It is especially significant that this loss was even greater in the years 1945 to 1948, when the so-called cold war was relatively mild, than in the years since 1948 with the mounting tension in Germany, Communist victory in China, aggression in Korea, and continued Congressional investigations.

What motives impel members to quit?

As in the case of the reasons why they join, the answer is not simple. No one factor can be assigned. But in general, the motives for both joining and leaving are to be found in the intangibles, in psychological development rather than in specific happenings. In this country the ideology which puts most stress on economics as the motivating force in society appeals least to the individual economic interest of Communist membership. As hope of gain seldom draws anyone into the party, a desire to earn more money seldom leads anyone to quit. Former members themselves say at first that they left because of some obnoxious twist in the party line or some specific incident which opened their eyes to the true nature of the party. But further talk reveals additional if not more basic motives.

Young people whose membership was a rebellion against a family situation mature emotionally and leave the party. Women and men, too, who fell in love with a Communist, fall out of love. The death of a lover in the party often coincides with immediate loss of interest in the "love" of all mankind. Those who sought to escape from the oppressive authority of a parent often in turn rebel against the oppressive authority of the party.

What happens to them emotionally and materially after they quit?

The most striking and general effects of departure from the Communist party are an increased standard of living and a real loneliness, coupled with an understandable fear of being smeared or discriminated against. The party blackmail system and the fear of McCarthyism keep them in the party and follow them even after they leave. Some continue to crusade for the ideals which they believe communism betrayed. Others wish only to avoid being involved in any controversial organization. But none seems to change much in personality. They often seem sincerely convinced that a change in their character has taken place. But as they go on talking or writing, they reveal themselves as being just like the French proverb, the more they change the more they are the same. Those who were cruel or bitter or timid or unable to accept the responsibilities of decision in a free world remain that way. So do those who were gentle or kind or aggressive or suspicious. But nearly all of them pass through a period of great loneliness as they cut themselves off from friends in the party— usually their only friends—and find it hard to win new ones.

Men and women who, as party members, were the most eager to vote for expulsion of a comrade suspected of talking to a Trotskyite or deviating in some other manner from the party line are the ones who are most eager to expose their former friends even if some of those friends also have left. On the other hand, those who in the party were willing to concede something to leniency are reluctant to "squeal" in public and even try to protect Communists they think are mere dupes.

The difficulties, both mental and material, which attend an escape from the party are well known to every member. This accounts for the long delay usually experienced between the desire to leave and the actual departure. This period may be years and almost always is measured in months. In fact, it would seem that on the average Communists spend one fourth of their time in the party nerving themselves to the point of getting out of it. Our societal attitudes keep them imprisoned.

How many former Communists are there in the United States?

Putting together all the best available estimates and checking these against the known membership of certain years as furnished by the FBI, we have reached the conclusion that some 700,000 men and women have left the Communist party in this country in the last 30 years. This is many more than most people seem to realize, for it is common to find the Communist membership of today exaggerated in popular fear and the turnover in membership minimized by the natural disinclination of most former Communists to parade the fact that they ever belonged.

This figure means that on the average the typical Communist is a party member for possibly two or three years. This is a rapid rate of turnover for any organization in America. It is more in keeping with the length of time national magazines hold the average subscription. Obviously these 700,000 are not hermits and are not starving. The great majority of them are working.

These conclusions may sound dogmatic, even arbitrary. We think that the evidence to support them will be found in the chapters that follow. If some of the statements appear to be startling or contradictory to accepted beliefs, it may be because everybody has been talking so hard about communism that they have forgotten to look at Communists.

~~~~~~~~~~~~~~~~~~~~~~~~~~~~~~~

CHAPTER TWO

PEOPLE WHO KNOW

THE best thing about the Communist party in America is the people who leave it. Not that former party members are heroes. But some have proved that they can be useful citizens, and they represent the best reservoir for an understanding fight against communism that we have. For they are people who know. They know what makes the party tick and what it takes to draw members out of it.

Approximately 300 of them have contributed to this book. They are a very mixed group, but whether they are completely typical of all Communists or former Communists, we do not presume to say. They are people who have been through the mill and are willing to offer their experience for what help they may be. The help they envisage ranges from destruction of communism root and branch to the gentle hope that there will be a better social order if more people understand, and that the young may be deterred from joining the party.

They come from all sections of the country and from all walks of life, although more of them were born and raised in cities than in the country and most of them are educated far above the average of our people. Both these facts seem to be true of Communists in general in this country. Some of them wrote out their stories at considerable length. Others prepared answers to a questionnaire with side comments. Still others were interviewed. Also the volumes of testimony of the various Congressional committees contained some material against which it was possible to check some of our own stories. Only once in a while a witness who was formerly a Communist was allowed to tell a little about his background, his reasons for joining the party, and his reasons for leaving. We found through 1951, 69 in all who told something of their background. A few, apparently determined to explain themselves fully, presented fairly extensive autobiographies. In most instances, the relevant detail is scant, for witnesses would be cut off before they could say very much, since this was not a type of information the interrogators desired. We have used these accounts sparingly, and where they are quoted in the later text, they will be identified.

While our collaborators, therefore, do not represent any scientific sampling of the total number of former Communists, for we were not trying to conduct a poll, they make up the largest collection of biographical sketches of former party members which we know about outside of the FBI files. The stories have been given to us under guarantee of anonymity for the tellers, and many under terms of professional secrecy. They naturally wanted to be assured that their words would not be quoted at them or held against them personally. If they can be assured of anonymity, they recount freely both the good and the bad they can remember. We found in writing a previous book (*For Better or Worse,* dealing with what happens to people after divorce) that men and women who have been through a profound experience want to tell about it as completely as they can. Furthermore, the fact that they tell it themselves makes the story more human and more easily understood than if it was related by someone else. Each of the persons interviewed told us about many other men and women still in the party or withdrawn from it. Thus the total of life stories serving as the basis for this book may amount to as many as a thousand case histories. In fact we could have covered several thousand more stories, but concluded that for our purposes after we had covered several hundred stories the new factors disclosed were scant and that additional interviews resulted only in further cumulative corroboration of the basic factors which had already been disclosed to us.

Do they tell the truth? We think they are telling it as they see it. Of course there is never any good corroborating evidence of motives, feelings, and beliefs in any man's account of his life or experiences. One judges often whether or not people are truthful by their manner, what they say, and how they say it. In addition our interviews were often so long and detailed as to make it difficult for anyone to answer in inconsistent terms. Above all it must be remembered that our collaborators have no reason to lie. They cannot thereby justify themselves in the eyes of the world, for they know that no one will identify them. To insure the promised anonymity, all the names used for these collaborators are fictitious (only when we quote from the public record mentioned above do we use real names), and in irrelevant detail we have made some changes to prevent identification. They have neither hope of reward nor fear of punishment. As for the notion that some of them might have been planted on us, that hardly seems reasonable. Neither Communists nor anti-Communists could conceivably gain anything by giving us a few purposely faked stories to distort the picture. They could not think we are that important. In short, from the circumstances under which we worked and our own experience in law and journalism at assessing the truth of factual reports, we believe the stories are as accurate as the tellers could make them.

This is not an attempt at amateur psychoanalysis. The autobiographical method is better in some respects, even if it may be less satisfactory in others. Sometimes the blind spots revealed are as enlightening as any remembered fact.

Most of them have agreed to participate in this project because they think it will contribute to the understanding and therefore to the defeat of this Russian-dominated party. Some of them are as belligerent as any red-baiter protected by the cloak of Congressional immunity. Some are still Marxists and a very few are believers in what might be called an American communism. Some are convinced that the best strategy is a subtle form of persuasion and education among the Communist rank and file.

In the first group, for example, is a man we will call Jim R—, a tough, middle-aged fighter who was self-educated and party-educated. He quit the party in 1932 and writes:

"I have fought the party bitterly for fifteen years and in my opinion there is only one way for an ex-Communist to redeem himself and that is to get stuck into the party and punch and keep on punching the bastards. They're not so tough—actually a cowardly bunch of yahoo men, and if a man has the intestinal fortitude to say a great big Boo! to them they stagger and wilt. They put on the character assassination smear, but if you know your stuff and have the brass in you to fight back, the yellow streak in them shows up.

"You can't fight them like gentlemen; you must give them dirt for dirt and plenty of it, in fact smother them in it. You have to out-fight them, out-roar them, out-curse them, and out-smear them."

Harry F— had been a Communist even longer than Jim, and is just as ardent an anti-Communist today. A writer born into a well-to-do Western family, he had been a youthful radical, then a sympathizer with the Russian revolution, then a Communist. It needed several years of inner struggle before he could bring himself to attack openly his former beliefs and former comrades. He has done it in his work unflinchingly, because he believes, as he wrote in his account of his life:

"Ex-Communists, and those fellow-travelers who studied Marxism-Leninism-Stalinism, are best equipped to combat communism."

We have been able to collect the first-person accounts of individuals who have left the party during the last 20 years or more. They start with some of the so-called Lovestoneites, followers of Jay Lovestone who as a young prodigy was one of the founders of the Communist movement in this country. When he left in 1929, the year Trotsky was expelled from Russia, a group of ardent Marxists went with him. Our collaborators represent the various exoduses ever since, right up to young people who quit in the fall of 1951.

Among the stories are several of husband-and-wife and several of brother-and-sister. There are also some of children who were virtually born into the party. Trained by parents who were careful to indoctrinate the youngsters with their own strict political slant from the beginning, they comprise a substantial number of the manual workers in our group of former Communists. Their break with the party, which usually occurred when they reached their early or middle twenties, was an even more painful experience than it was to others, for they had never known any other way of life and were cutting themselves off completely from their families. In fact they rejected at the same time their own parents and their adopted father Stalin and adopted mother Russia. Most of the others were returning to a remembered way of life and to their families.

One of these children of communism, the son of parents born on the shore of the Baltic, may be called Stephen Z. He is still thoroughly leftist by conviction, but confesses to a sense of shame at having been "taken in" for so long by the Communists. At the same time, he hesitated for two years before he quietly dropped out of party activities, and he writes:

"I feared my family. As a matter of fact, to this day they don't know I actually don't belong or rather don't believe in the 'party' any more."

Among the workers, whether they were brought up to communism as children or joined later, there seems to have been less concealment of party membership than among the white-collar and professional groups. This seems to be more like the European Communist parties which have much larger labor memberships. In France, for example, there are some 4,000,000 workers who at one time or another belonged to the Communist party, made no bones about it, and are rather more proud than otherwise of having left it.

Most of the former Communists who contributed to this book were rank-and-file members, although a few held a variety of official positions ranging from very minor to medium and several had been selected for posts of secondary leadership. None of them is among the former Communists who made a great public parade of their communism, either through writing books about it or appearing repeatedly on the witness stand in sensational cases, whether in court or before Congressional investigators, and capitalizing on the experience. We sought the unheralded rank-and-file members because we believed

that it was among them rather than the exceptional personality that we would find answers to our questions about
communism and Communists in the United States.

Both of us have met some of the leaders of communism
in this country over the years, one of us as a lawyer and
the other as a newspaperman. Not only are they not in
character or personality of the "masses" they want to subvert, but they are consciously apart from the body of their
own membership. They regard themselves as an "elite" in
an elite party. Having met them, we became more interested in their followers.

It might be supposed that these followers, once they have
decided not to follow the party line any longer, simply
would resign or drop out. But it is not as easy as that. Part
of the difficulty no doubt is personal, but both the party
and the rest of society account for even more.

The party itself does not hesitate to resort to blackmail
and persecution. They will see that the "deserter" is
denounced anonymously as a Communist or even as a spy
to his employer; he will be ostracized by other members
and since party work usually cuts him off from those he
knew before joining, he is lonely. With the loneliness
goes fear. The rest of society is not too eager to welcome the
prodigal, even if there are no doubts as to his sincerity.
There may be more joy over one repentant sinner in
heaven than over many righteous men, but that is in
heaven. On earth the joy is severely limited.

Thus we find Bill, a sensitive actor from the South,
recalling:

"After I got out of the CP, I experienced considerable
difficulty in getting a job. It took months. I was slandered
by the Communist press as a Fascist, a liaison between
Trotsky and Franco. Today, I can laugh this off; then, it
was exceedingly painful."

Even when a job is not an important factor, there are other distressing features in leaving the party. Mary L., a housewife from the Northwest who had belonged to the party for two years before her marriage, was a city-government secretary. She writes:

"I know that it would be difficult to find employment were I to seek it because of my one-time association with the party [which ended more than ten years ago]. Fortunately, I have not had to do so.

"In my own case, newspaper publicity, false and otherwise, relative to my past party membership has been personally distressing—both in fact and in anticipation—as have been frequent inquiries on the part of FBI agents wanting to obtain information concerning persons who were, or were thought to have been, members of the party at the same time as I. These inquiries began in 1948 in connection with the federal loyalty program.

"In addition to appearing before the Dies subcommittee in 1940 [after she quit the party], I have been called as a witness before a Congressional Investigating Committee, before a Federal Grand Jury and have been a government witness in a federal perjury trial. I have known real fear on and before all of these occasions—excruciating, terrifying fear. One is not permitted, as of 1950-51 particularly, to forget his past."

Then there is the experience of George A. and his wife, Helen, both of whom had been Communists and decided to leave the party together. Although they had an income apart from his job, it was not enough to support them as they had been living, and George writes of this part of their experience:

"I know the company would have fired me if they had known that I had been a member. This, even though the product we made had no relation to the military aspects of our government. Night after night we considered how we should move against the potential threat of blackmail held by the party. As you know, they write anonymous letters to the employer, identifying ex-members in order to have them fired. In this respect they are really as bad as McCarthy. . . . You know that in the Manual there are specific instructions for making life miserable for ex-members and that this goes even to the point of harassing the children of ex-members by putting marks and evil words on their doors, desks in schools, etc."

These expressions could be multiplied. Whether fear or loneliness is worse, a break with the party in this country cannot now be made easily, except in a minority of cases.

In spite of their difficulties, however, most of the former Communists we have encountered are working (and doing better at it than when they were party members) and seem to be more content in their domestic relationships than before. While most of them are eager to explain how communism could be opposed successfully and to continue to fight for the genuinely liberal ideals which they say led them to join the party, a substantial minority want nothing except to be let alone. They do not want to fight communism; they do not want to join anything for any reason; they do not wish to be noticed. Here are some typical expressions from different people:

"I am afraid of all movements now; I won't join anything."

"When I resigned, I did not join some other movement; in fact, I have been extremely cautious in joining anything that was not entirely reputable."

"I pull punches in discussing things with some people."

And a veteran of the Spanish Civil War's Lincoln Brigade, who tried to organize other members against the Communist line after the fall of France in 1940, reports that a vast majority of the hundreds of men he talked to said:

"I'm through with the party but count me out." This veteran adds:

"They were not neutral on the issue; on the contrary, they were bitter about it, but they wouldn't express it in action."

Some of the former members obviously miss the companionship, the sense of belonging, the excitement, and the work which the party gave them. Few of them had been happy people before they joined, and found at best a synthetic joy that comes from action or what seemed to be action while they were in. Not many of them have been happy since they left, although some have found real contentment.

In collecting these stories, we have been indebted to more than one source. During the course of our work, we have been asked how we could gather several times more histories than the Congressional committees have exposed in the last dozen years. One answer is that the Congressional committees did not try very hard; they were not interested in the former Communist except as an informer or a scapegoat. So even without the power of subpoena or investigative funds, it was easier for us.

A few of these collaborators were known to one or the other of us. But the great majority came to us as one former Communist told another of what we were trying to do. A few more came in as the result of publicity about our plans. A few more stories were sent to us as the result of an article we wrote for *The New Leader* explaining our project, and still others after appearance on the *Herald-Tribune* forum.

To each former member we explained that we had no preconceived ideas for which we wanted support. We did want to know what their family background had been, what led them to join the party, what phases of the experience repelled and attracted, what the benefits had been or the hardships, what impelled them to leave and what happened afterward. We were interested in the persons who they thought influenced them both in joining and leaving as well as any specific propaganda or event. We wanted to know whether Papa voted for Herbert Hoover or for Debs, whether brothers and sisters were rivals or companions, whether they had many friends or few.

We told them we hoped they would write about their feelings in regard to the secrecy of the party, the rigidity of the dogma, the work assigned them as party members. We asked for the age at which they joined, how long it took them to make up their minds to leave, the manner of their leaving—whether by resignation, expulsion, or just dropping out.

Those who offered to cooperate were asked also to describe their experiences in leaving and afterward. Did they make their departure known to family and friends? Did they find it embarrassing? Did they have trouble getting a job? Were they harassed by former comrades? Did they join other movements and if so what kind? Did they experience intolerance from the non-Communist world? Did they have to make a whole new life or were they able to continue much as they had been?

To each we wrote that our purpose was "to give a fuller understanding to the American people of why Americans of all people on this earth of ours join the Communist party, and more specifically, why they leave, and the difficulties of the divorce."

We undertook to provide complete protection as to anonymity. We hoped, therefore, that the accounts written or told would be frank and as accurate as it is possible for a man to be in speaking about himself. Complete objectivity is hardly to be expected in any autobiography. But every man knows more facts about himself than anyone else can; he may have difficulty in expressing his knowledge and assaying the facts or even acting on them. But he has a near-monopoly over the initial material.

Out of this information, it seemed to us, would come some basis for at least tentative conclusions on the nature of the Communist and the best way to combat him or save him. It would explain, at least in part, some of the puzzling features of the extremist, which is what every Communist must be. Furthermore, he is a rather special type of extremist, one who can swing from one extreme to another with remarkable facility. The Communist, for example, must be able to hail a comrade as "Hero of the People" today and be ready to revile him as a "Mad Dog Trotskyite" tomorrow. Furthermore, he must be able to do both at the behest of a party superior whether or not a reasonable explanation is provided. In America, he must be so far from sharing the fairly common American fault of deprecating foreigners that he is content to accept the contemptuous direction of foreigners, and especially Russians. Is this willingness to be treated like backward children related to a trait observed in some Anglophiles of loving to be insulted by a British peer?

The millions of dollars, millions of man-hours, millions of pages of print that have been expended to fight communism in the United States have seldom been directed toward finding the answers to this sort of question. We have learned of only one serious study of the Communist personality in this country. This one is being conducted at Princeton. It is a project for a detailed, careful, elaborate, deep analysis of 50 American ex-Communists by eminently qualified specialists in various fields. It will be correlated with analyses of similar groups in several other countries. When the results are completed, more answers to the questions we have suggested can be expected.

This lack of scientific inquiry contrasts with a wealth of research into the psychology of murderers, rapists, thieves, arsonists, embezzlers, and even of bigots and fanatics in other areas than communism. Many unreasoning haters of the Soviet system would say this is all we need. They lump the Communist in with the criminal and let it go at that. But it is obvious that the similarity is more in the neurosis of the hater of communism than in reality.

The manner in which our collaborators brought out the workings of the mind that led them into and out of communism was convincing evidence that psychology rather than economics is the strength of the Communist party in America. That being so, it would follow that one of the most powerful weapons to combat the party would be the weapons of psychological warfare. The experiences related in the following chapters, and those already published by other ex-Communists, should be the foundation for expert research to give us the raw material to forge these weapons.

Of course we do not suggest that all Communists follow a single pattern, psychologically or otherwise. In fact, we are sure this is not so. There are no characteristics which mark them as totally different from other Americans. As one of the men whose own story is in this book wrote to us in irritating fashion:

"It seems to me that there is no more reason for Communists as a group to be motivated by the Oedipus complex than for liberals as a group, including yourselves."

This man, the offspring of a better-than-average income family, and a life-long student, had made his own approach to communism on what he regarded and still regards as coldly rational grounds. He was one of those who saw in himself and others chiefly "simple motivations like looking for an intellectual solution to economic problems, striving to do away with world war, and seeking the betterment of one's country and mankind."

But no man's motives are quite that simple. They are complicated by the frequently obscure and almost unknown influences which made this son of a well-to-do family a Communist while other rich men's sons equally intelligent, equally desirous of peace and justice, fought for their ideals through other channels. The network of influences which mold the lives and minds of Communists in America is difficult to untangle, but it exists with some clarity in broad general terms.

Communists are a part of the whole American mass of dissenters, nonconformists. The strength of our nation lies in part in its resistance to conformity. There is a special category within this large and extremely valuable group. In probing into the reasons for a Communist, it must never be forgotten that some of the world's greatest men and women are violently dissenting rebels, and that some of the triumphs of progress have been achieved through a stubborn nonconformity. Clemenceau is supposed to have said: Any man who is not a Socialist at 25 has no heart and any man who is a Socialist at 60 has no brain.

The Communist dissenter, however, is not nearly so much of an individualist as most nonconformists. The Communist justifies his desire to accept decisions made by others rather than make them himself, or to participate in the making of them, by the plea that is the only road to the ultimate goal of a better society. But the real reason seems to be the desire for a haven where the Communists will have a guide to action and thought under all circumstances. Most other nonconformists rather revel in the absence of such a guide even when they are on occasion willing to accept the decisions of others. This difference was so obvious in so many of the men and women who talked and wrote to us that it must be fairly common. The Communist party is one of the most admirable refuges for such a personality because there is always a guide— Stalin or the latest word on the party line from Moscow or even the instructions given by a minor official at the last cell meeting.

The complexity of the motives and personality traits which prompt resignation from the party is as tangled as that which led to joining. Nearly always there is an obvious and reasonable cause for quitting. But less clear though not less powerful explanations emerge from further study of most cases.

As the Communist drive for world power has revealed itself in one or another aspect that has seemed shameful to Westerners, there have been successive waves of withdrawal from the United States party. Those in each wave profess themselves as quite unable to understand how anyone who is untainted by treasonable thought could possibly wait until later to leave. The big dramatic moments which gave so many Communists their exit cues were highly publicized all over the world. Yet in actual fact the desertions from the party seem to have been almost as numerous in quieter years. The dramatic moments remain in the memories of both the former Communists and the public.

A highly successful lawyer in an Eastern city had been a member of the party for several years before the purge of old Bolsheviks in Russia placed Stalin in a position of undisputed power. The lawyer, who has a nice sense of justice in other matters, is extremely bitter in his unqualified denunciations of anyone who left the party later than he did. He can justify his own membership to himself by repeating that he got out when the true nature of the party was revealed. He feels that he cleansed himself by his wisdom in recognizing the truth, but fails to see how anyone could remain a dupe after the purge. This man also justified the precise moment of his joining and is disdainful of those who joined after he did.

A happily married housewife of culture and education was a firm believer in the unfortunate necessity of the purges. She was sure the old Bolsheviks had betrayed the revolution as certainly as Benedict Arnold had betrayed that of 1776. She left the party when the Stalin-Hitler pact was announced. Now she sneers at anyone who could have remained in the party at a later date.

One young veteran who joined the party while studying under the GI Bill of Rights had his eyes opened, he says, by the development of the cold war. It seemed to him that the twistings of Soviet policy and the refusal of the Russians to cooperate in reasonable attempts to establish peace showed any person of good will that the protestations of the party in this country were a fake. He could understand membership based on admiration for Russia's share in the war; he could not see remaining in the party after revelations of espionage and non-cooperation.

But another young man of somewhat similar background, who became a teacher after his graduation from college, remained in the party until the Communist attack in Korea. That for him was the payoff. He had managed the mental acrobatics of the party line up to that moment; no one but a dupe or a traitor, he says, could have done it any longer.

He would have nothing but scorn, if he knew her, for another young teacher who swallowed without difficulty the line that the Communists were fighting a war of libera-

tion in Korea. She used her savings and her 1951 vacation
to attend the party's youth peace conference in Berlin.
(Her school board thought she was touring France and
Italy, incidentally.) The phony nature of that meeting,
she tells us, led to her retirement from the party after she
came home. She left with some fear that she would be
betrayed by fellow members, and wanted advice on whether
she should tell her principal about her former membership. She was desperately afraid of losing her job if she
told, and of losing it if she didn't because some Communist
would betray her.

This fear of leaving the party is very real for many, and
not without reason. Every party member seems to know
that the party itself has informed on deserters or those
it has expelled. The ostracism, social and business, which
has dogged many a former Communist who was unable or
unwilling to provide a dramatic story of secret Communists
in key places is also well known. In our accounts, there
is a recurrent undertone of this fear. It explains why so
often there is a delay of months or even years between
the decision to quit the party and the actual departure.

The purpose behind understanding the Communist and
what makes him join or leave the party is more than alle-
viation of our own fears. With knowledge of these factors,
we can act on them to reduce the party membership more
drastically than harsh repressive measures possibly can.

The broad base of the party is its rank and file. These
are the people who join labor unions and all kinds of civic
organizations, seeking to gain enough influence to sway
the whole group. These are the people who give the party
its outward show of strength and do a good deal of the recruiting of new members. They are not and never have
been numerous at any one time.

The exact membership is unknown to the public for any

year before 1949 and 1950, when the figures were compiled and announced by the FBI. They were 54,174 for 1949 and 43,217 for 1950. By the end of 1951 the figure was put at 31,608. Since the Communist party has been driven underground, we may expect membership figures and other statistical information to be increasingly more difficult to obtain and more unreliable. The peak membership of more than 100,000 was reached during the time of our war alliance with Russia. If we take the FBI figures along with the most authentic estimates available for the 23 years back to 1929, we find the *average* membership has been about 40,000. Before 1929 the public figures are too vague to have much meaning, but certainly seem to have been smaller on the average than 40,000. Throughout the years, the hard core of leaders and what might be called professionals has been about 5,000 to 8,000.

If the lessons of the past, and especially the stories of former members, were conned intelligently, we are convinced that the rank and file of the Communist party under 30 years old could be sucked out so fast that communism in the United States would be reduced to that hard core. The FBI could deal unaided with these. They might constitute a danger in espionage and sabotage. They would cease to be a menace through subversion.

CHAPTER THREE

THIRTY YEARS' WAR

On A cold day of 1919 in Paris, three elderly gentle-men who were making what the world hoped would be a permanent peace got around to discussing Russia. It was even colder in Siberia where puzzled American soldiers found themselves involved in Russia's civil war. The elderly gentlemen—President Wilson, Prime Minister Lloyd George, Premier Clemenceau—were as confused by the Bolshevik Revolution as the soldiers in Siberia.

Wilson, frankly bewildered by conflicting and inadequate reports of what went on behind the curtain which Russia seems able to pull before herself so easily, thought it might be wise to recognize the fact that the Bolsheviks were the actual rulers of the state. Lloyd George was willing, but members of his own cabinet led by Winston Churchill insisted on trying to throw the Communist rascals out of Moscow, and it was not an issue on which the Prime Minister wished to risk his government. Clemenceau refused even to meet a Bolshevik, threatening to resign if one were invited to Paris. None of the smaller countries were any more eager than the Frenchman to meet the Communist leaders.

"It was as if I had proposed that we should invite a delegation of lepers from the stricken isle of Molokai," Lloyd George said.

The little Welshman, one of the most astute politicians of his time, described in that sentence the nature of the fight we have been waging against communism ever since. It has been a fight based on fear and unfamiliarity, very much like the fear and ignorance which governed medieval reactions to the dreaded plague. Men who did not know how the disease infected people could only devise fantastically foolish measures to combat it and could take no steps to prevent it. So with communism.

In this country there had been great sympathy with the Russian Revolution. The two countries, despite diametrically opposite forms of government, had exchanged good offices ever since Russia had helped prevent a European coalition to support the Confederacy during our Civil War, a most unusual step in international relations. Congress had passed resolutions deploring pogroms in a spirit of real friendship for the Russian people. Average American newspaper readers were as pleased to hear that Russians had been liberated from their Czarist oppressors as were most Siberian exiles. These readers, even more poorly informed about Russian events than Wilson, became hostile to the Bolsheviks only when Russia made a separate peace with Germany, allowing fresh German divisions to be released against the Western Front. It was only later that we began to discover sources of danger in the Communist Manifesto. Most of us really knew little about this document, prepared in candlelight by Marx and Engels 70 years earlier. We had been afraid of the ideas expressed in it, and our fears magnified them and gave us no chance to answer them. The attempts at censorship or suppression of the manifesto produced the usual results of censorship—

fear of the suppressed and ignorance as to techniques to do battle with the ideas expressed.

Now that the war was won anyway, the three gentlemen in Paris were looking for a way out. But because they could not agree, they did nothing jointly and two months later the Bolsheviks launched their Third International with a manifesto calling for the world revolution and offering material and moral aid to Communist movements everywhere or anywhere. At about the same time Herbert Hoover was writing to Wilson:

"We have also to contemplate what would actually happen if [in reply] we undertook military intervention. We should probably be involved in years of police duty, and our first act would probably in the nature of things make us a party to the Allies to re-establishing the reactionary classes . . . we would find ourselves subordinated and even committed to policies against our convictions."

Herbert Hoover hoped to substitute food for force, but his plan failed and the first great wave of fear of communism swept across Europe and into America.

In Europe where new nations were being carved out of old despotisms and monarchies were dying dramatically, the fear that revolution might not stop short of communism was very real. In the United States where revolutionary zeal immediately after the war was devoted chiefly to liquor, sex, and mass production, the fright was less reasonable but just as acute. It found an expression in the hysterical witch hunt conducted by Wilson's Attorney General, A. Mitchell Palmer, before the days the FBI was headed by J. Edgar Hoover. There was an accompanying wave of ugly opportunism as ruthless men used the hysteria of the moment to smash labor unions and silence outspoken liberals. A few Communists were deported or sent to jail, along with hundreds of non-Communist foreigners.

The unsavory episode gave the new Communist party of the United States a fine start, supplying cheap martyrdom and identifying the movement with some highly respected people and some very popular reforms.

This opening gambit of armed intervention abroad and frightened or calculated red-baiting at home set the pattern for anti-Communist activities in the United States. It is a pattern that has persisted through more than 30 years. It is worth recalling the main battles in this strange war, if only to pave the way for more effective strategy.

The year 1919 saw the birth of two Communist groups in the United States—the Communist party and the Communist Labor party. Merged the following year, and kept underground by the Palmer tactics, the Communist party appeared to be a far more formidable conspiracy than it really was. That is what scared people. Yet there never has been a time when the FBI did not have agents inside the party, and that these agents were entirely familiar with the party secrets and plans is proved by the many volumes of memoirs they have written since. A great many of the early leaders, spotted by these agents, have long since left the Communist ranks; many others are dead. The accounts written, even with the advantage of hindsight, by those who attended their public and secret meetings show that the movement was largely one of talk, ideological disputes, and vague plans allegedly for organizing so-called workers.

The party thrived on attempts at suppression. When Michigan passed a criminal syndicalist law aimed at Communists, the party called a meeting of leaders on an isolated farm at Bridgman, and had the satisfaction of being raided by the FBI and deputy sheriffs. The resulting trials under the state law were wonderful propaganda for communism. It is always difficult for Americans, recalling the origin of our own country, to think that revolution against intolerable conditions is anything but good. It is equally difficult for a people nurtured on traditions of free speech to get too angry at even violent talk. Yet the people of Michigan were sufficiently alarmed that a jury convicted Charles Ruthenberg, secretary of the party. Another jury, less excited, disagreed over the party's then (and present) head, William Z. Foster. Ruthenberg died before the Supreme Court passed on his appeal, which impartial lawyers believe he might have won, and after 11 years the cases against the rest of those netted in the raid were dismissed.

In those days fear of communism as a danger to American life was joined by fear of communism as a foe of American privilege. In fact, Communists were then as now chiefly interested in abuses as a means of rising to power themselves rather than in practical corrective measures. The result was that people who were not afraid of reform tended to minimize the more soundly based objections to communism. Even more important, the fears prevented any real understanding of Communist procedures or the Communist appeal.

Against all evidence, it was constantly being shouted that these dangerous people were aliens, Jews, Negroes, and dissatisfied workers. The alien-membership angle persisted, and is repeated in a recent book by one of the earliest FBI agents engaged in anti-Communist activity. Yet the names he mentions are in great majority those of native-born white Americans with more than a worker's education. There are only about as many Jews as you might expect to find in any group with a membership largely confined to large cities, as is the case with communism.

The fears generated by the Palmer raids did not die, but the hysteria could hardly be maintained at fever pitch for 30 years. It flared up again in the years during which Stalin was overthrowing Trotsky, this particular phase coming to a head in the refusal of the United States to give political asylum to the loser when Trotsky was exiled early in 1929.

These years also marked the beginning of periodic defections from the Communist ranks. While the membership was overwhelmingly native, the party leaders always took their orders from the Soviet headquarters. Successive waves of converts to communism have joined the movement or the party and left it after some specific example of Russian domineering or a general dissatisfaction with foreign orders. The Trotskyites were one notable wave, but the highly colored accounts of their leader's quarrel with Stalin led to a national fear of them even greater at times than that felt for the party rulers. For Trotsky was said to have broken with Stalin because Stalin would not go all-out for world revolution but wished first to consolidate Russia's strength. Therefore, we were afraid to admit to the country a man who for many years was regarded in the Kremlin as its Public Enemy Number One.

The depression provided another irrational fear of communism. Because Communists talked a great deal about economic problems, it was taken for granted that the party had an economic base, and the rising millions of unemployed under the regime of Herbert Hoover were supposed to be easy pickings for Communist propaganda. Perhaps decades or generations of such misery, without hope of betterment, would have attracted masses of workers as was the case in some European and Asiatic countries, where the Communist appeal of land and bread was strong. They could not even make such an appeal in the United States, for talk of an acre or two of land would have been mockery to farmers who owned or sharecropped 80 or more but could not make a living.

Of course the Communists did gain from the depression, especially from the newly poor, and there were very many frightened people among their enemies. But none of these people thought to institute a study of what kind of recruits the Communists were getting, why they joined, and what they wanted. Nor was this situation improved when fear of the rising fascism of Europe was added to the fear of communism. Confusion was compounded as some prayed that Stalin would wipe out the Nazis, and others that Hitler would destroy the Soviet Communist regime. Both were dismayed when Hitler and Stalin signed a pact of friendship. Few people had noted the affinity between communism and fascism, even though both groups played together in the early days of Hitler in Germany. Communism here revived when Russia became our ally in the war against Germany.

The fears and confusions are best seen in the careers of the Congressional committees established in the thirties and still continuing to investigate un-American activities. These committees were far less concerned with the menace of fascism than with that of communism, but they did not do a very good job of helping us understand either. The fundamental fault was a failure to study the real reasons people joined, the kind of people they were, or the best methods of getting them out.

This failure prevented us from making the most of the blows that were struck against communism here by the very policies of Russia. The great purges of the thirties brought thousands out of the United States party. The Hitler-Stalin pact and the Russian attack on Finland disillusioned more thousands who had believed that anti-Nazi and propeace statements by the Soviet leaders were based on principle. Hitler's attack on Russia in the summer of 1941 caused the pendulum to swing back for communism in the United States. Soviet popularity as an ally helped the party throughout the war. It began to suffer defections again when it became clear that Russia would not cooperate with the West in establishing peace. This process was hastened further by the Communist attack in Korea.

Meanwhile the biggest battle against communism was being waged in American labor unions, a battle in which labor leaders and some wise employers joined forces. The determined drive of the party to infiltrate and control key unions, which had been immeasurably strengthened by the Roosevelt New Deal, was the most successful effort Communists made in this country. Their victories were achieved in part through discipline, financial strength, skill, and ruthlessness rather than numbers. They were aided enormously by reactionaries who tried to pin the Communist label on causes and policies with which 90 per cent of the American people agreed. When collective bargaining or antidiscrimination laws or public housing or adequate relief or health insurance are denounced as Communist aims, people who approve of these things and know they themselves are not Communist find it difficult to fight communism vigorously. Nothing has played into the hands of the Communists so greatly as the readiness of red-baiters to allow and even help Communists to monopolize good works and good measures, especially when this is coupled with the timidity of liberals who are in favor of the reforms but refrain from denouncing Communist infiltration.

Aided by their unconscious allies among the reactionaries in the Republican party and among the Southern Democrats, tiny groups of Communists were able to capture or nearly capture unions with tens of thousands of members. Joseph Curran, head of the Maritime Union, for instance, after winning the long battle to drive Communists from control, tells us that there never were more than 300 Communist party members in the union at any one time. The biggest estimate of actual Communist card holders in the movie industry at any one time was 200 out of 30,000 men and women who work in that industry in Hollywood.

It should be no surprise that a small number of people working closely together should be able to control a large organization. Most of us have seen this happen in the clubs or civic organizations to which we belong. A very few active members really run the show. Big corporations and mutual companies are proud of the number of their stockholders or members. But a handful of men at the top exercise real control. The Metropolitan Life Insurance Company, for example, is a mutual enterprise with millions of members—that is to say, policy holders. Yet less than a score of them dominate it and perpetuate themselves in power over billions of dollars of assets.

A disciplined minority, however small, can and usually does control a disorganized majority. Many laws, such as that setting up the Securities and Exchange Commission to regulate the intricate system of corporate finance, have been passed in part to protect the rights of majorities against the oppression of minorities. In fact, in many fields it is much more necessary to provide protection for the great unorganized majority of the people than for the dominating minority.

The tactics of the Communists in seizing control of some unions, therefore, were not new. They worked hard, fought for or took credit for the things rank-and-file members most wanted in the way of progress and security, and they also promoted each other tirelessly. One Communist in a key position would disparage the work of non-Communists and praise his fellow party members in the union. They were able to infiltrate into positions of power all the more easily because throughout this era the enemies of labor smeared as Communists all union leaders who fought for their men.

Non-Communist labor leaders, partly because they were so close to the enemy, were the most effective American warriors against communism. They learned enough of the truth to win not only against the Communists in control but against the unconscious rightist allies of those Communists. Professional anti-Communists and former Communists, if these entered the fight because of the publicity they could get—as was the case with many—were of little help.

This struggle for the labor unions came very close to success. In the early forties the Communists controlled enough constituent unions in the CIO to have captured the whole organization if the non-Communist executives led by Philip Murray had not been wise. As it was, the party exercised so much control that during at least one Executive Committee meeting in Philadelphia, the CIO's general counsel, Lee Pressman, carried an advance galley proof of the proposed resolutions to the hotel room of Roy Hudson, Communist party Executive Committee member in charge of trade-union relations, and stealthily took back to the CIO Executive Committee changes which Hudson made. Hudson also told the Furriers, the Public Office Workers, and the Electrical Workers how to vote on such matters as the second front and support of Willkie against Franklin D. Roosevelt. Murray and his followers were wise enough not to press the issue of communism until they were sure they could win, which involved a period of education and organization work.

It should be noted that they broke the Communist hold

on labor by exposing the true nature of the Communist leadership's aims and the background of their support. It was not done by trying to take away the Communist's right to hold a job or even to campaign openly for the suppression of his views in union matters.

It is also significant that the job of exposing Communist leadership in unions was achieved, principally by labor itself, before the Taft-Hartley Law sought to outlaw Communist officials in unions. It was easy for a Communist official to give up his party card and say he was no longer a party member. But hard fighting by union members rather than Congressional action or legal requirements of oaths gave back control of the unions to non-Communists.

One other area of American life in which Communists had some success was the capture of organizations with large non-Communist memberships devoted to peace, to fighting fascism, to combating segregation and discrimination, to organizing consumers, etc. Americans, a race of joiners, were usually ready to suppose that an organization was designed for the purpose of its title. When the Communists either founded such groups or infiltrated and captured them, they could enjoy the front of many respectable non-Communist believers in the particular cause. It required eternal vigilance to detect the point at which Communists took over what may have been a strong and worthy organization, or to determine which new groups were actually Communist-dominated.

As an example of how easily traps could be set, one of the authors of this book was invited to address a large meeting on a subject in which he is known to believe strongly. The name of the sponsoring organization was new to him.

"Well, Mr. Ernst," he was told, "the presiding officer will be Newbold Morris."

Newbold Morris' views were sufficiently well known to inspire an acceptance, but a few minutes later Mr. Morris himself called.

"What is this organization that has asked me to preside?" he asked. "They tell me you are to be the main speaker, so I suppose it is all right."

Of course it turned out to be all wrong, and prospective speaker and presiding officer sent in their refusals to have anything to do with the meeting. But often this simple strategy is successful in gaining a new front for a Communist objective.

Part of the Communist strategy is further served when the people who are so fooled, or the people who belonged to a Communist-controlled organization before it was so controlled, are held up to public obloquy as Communists themselves. Yet this has been one of the favorite means of "combating" communism. "Counterattack" is a sample of an agency adding to our utter confusion and furthering the obnoxious principles of economic attainder.

Most Americans, little informed on the battles waged by labor and liberal organizations to get away or keep from Communist control, or of the activities of the FBI which are necessarily secret, have supposed that the Congressional investigations have been the principal front for the war against communism. The press, more interested in bad than good news, played up an accusation by a committee against one man rather than a union victory over a Communist gang in control.

Oldest of the committees in this field is the House Committee on un-American Activities, founded in 1936 and headed successively by Representatives Dies, Thomas, and Wood. It was preceded, however, by two shorter-lived committees. One, created by a House resolution in 1930, was under the chairmanship of Hamilton Fish and was exclusively directed against communism. Its caliber may be indicated by noting that one of its chief findings was that the American Civil Liberties Union was a Communist bulwark because of its activities on behalf of freedom of speech, press, and assembly. The second, created in 1934 with John W. McCormack as chairman, investigated Nazi activities even more than Communist, and did most of its work in executive session. It turned up a good deal of evidence on the financing of Nazi propaganda in the United States. Dies, the first chairman of the Un-American Activities Committee, preferred the example of Fish, although at the outset he had said:

"We might jeopardize fundamental rights far more important than the objective we seek."

After 13 years of the committee's work, this sounds prophetic. As a sounding board for professional harriers of dissent, who like to brand everyone they disagree with as Communist, and as an example, for the most part, of how not to combat communism, the committee has had no equal. Yet in its earlier days, although its stupidities shocked the conscience of those who think the Bill of Rights is the matrix of our Constitution, it was not without compassion. Members did more often express hope that the witness, who admitted having been a member of something accused of being red or even of being a former Communist, would not be fired from his job. Later investigating committees and later sessions of this committee give the impression that they are interested chiefly in two things: names of more Communists and former Communists, and evidence that membership is of foreign origin. They also seem to think in most cases it is part of their duty to make outcasts of anyone who admits ever having been a Communist or Communist sympathizer. At no time was there any real work done to discover, for example, the source of the millions of dollars flowing into the Communist party coffers.

The committee's search was maintained during the period of our war alliance with Russia. It had been made illegal for a Communist to hold a government job, and while the committees and investigators found a few party followers who were dismissed, the chief effect was a constant harassment of liberals or suspected liberals in government. Says former Attorney General Francis Biddle:

"If a single cause was responsible for the spread of the doctrine of guilt by association, linked with the growing doubt of the people about the loyalty of their public servants, and the strength of their traditional institutions, I should be tempted to find it in the activities of this committee."

After the war, the cleavage between Russia and the United States became so clear that it no longer was possible to mistake the Communist party for anything except a Soviet tool. Of course those who had observed this fact earlier tend to think there is no excuse for anyone being fooled any later than they were. But the fact is that the split was by no means so obvious or final until the period of reconstruction of the postwar world.

This was when the Thirty Years' War of fear and hysteria began to penalize American policy both at home and abroad. With our background of misconceptions, fright, and ignorance, we were in no position to meet the enemy, especially the enemy at home. As we entered the cold war, we had against the Communist party of the United States only the weapons bequeathed to us by Wilson and Palmer. Those weapons have been wielded by the McCarthys with tremendous political power and occasional skill. The only trouble is that the weapons are completely powerless against communism in America, having about the same effect as a bow and arrow against a tank.

This futile warfare has led us to the ultimate absurdity of attempting to legislate an idea out of existence, to defeat a philosophy with force, to set up a test oath to destroy people who believe an oath is a frivolity of capitalist or bourgeois morality. We have even had the naïve idea of fighting communism by outlawing the name of the political party. All they would do is change the name. They did just that on one occasion. We have solemnly asked the enemies within our gates to step up and register as pariahs. We have acted as if we really supposed that a man who will commit treason would not stoop to perjury. We have driven a group of conspirators underground, although the easiest way to destroy a conspiracy is to place it in the limelight. And we have done this in the face of protest from the head of the one organization which has collected some intelligent data on Communists in America. J. Edgar Hoover of the FBI has wisely said repeatedly that the task of defeating communism at home is hampered greatly by outlawing the party.

We know that Communists were doing more than we could see when they were a legal entity, and what we could not see scared us. So instead of taking steps to reveal that which was hidden, we have adopted measures which hide that which we formerly saw. It is as if we tried to make icebergs less dangerous to navigation by submerging them completely instead of allowing one seventh to show above the water.

Take the matter of money. The Communists through various devices have raised enormous sums in this country, probably far more than they ever received in "Moscow gold." The members of the party are everlastingly assessed, everlastingly egged on to collect for Communist enterprises. Wealthy Americans have contributed, as other wealthy Americans have contributed to the extremist conspirators of fascism in this country, and have been able to defy public opinion only because their names are not revealed. The Communists, for example, raised a million dollars ostensibly to fight the Scottsboro case, on which they spent $60,000. During the days of the Hitler-Stalin pact, they embarked upon a "Yanks Are Not Coming" picketing of the White House that was costing at the rate of $50,000 a year, the job being financed mainly by a few individuals whose names the public never knew.

The Communists would join forces with Gerald L. K. Smith, the so-called Committee on Constitutional Government, the National Association of Manufacturers, and a thousand embattled lobbies to maintain the privacy of contributions to their various organizations. Those who are protecting bigots and lobbyists are the leaders in preventing us from discovering the financial backing of communism.

We consider sacred the right of any of these people, including Communists, to contribute to any organization they like. But we consider equally sacred the right of the public, which is affected, to know who is giving money to what. Gerald L. K. Smith received 50 contributions of $5,000 or more in one single year. When the President's Civil Rights Committee saw the list, it came out unanimously for disclosure of the source of funds of all organizations which seek to influence the public. Disclosure might have cut Smith off from most if not all of these big givers—unless they had the courage to take a public position in favor of the beliefs they financed. It might do the same to the Communists. At least the givers would have to stand up and openly avow their support of the cause to which they give.

But more dangerous than our lack of knowledge about Communist funds is our lack of knowledge about Communists themselves. The Congressional committees, the private anti-Communist organizations, even the professions that should care the most, have failed to delve into the personalities and the backgrounds of party members. Our Thirty Years' War against communism has brought us back to the point at which we started.

In the following chapters we present material on which, we believe, a new departure can and should be based. It is offered for the consideration of all those who believe our aim should be the weakening of communism and the conversion of Communists rather than the use of the Communist menace to promote personal prejudices, personal ambitions, and national hysteria.

We have not quoted all the stories we received, but we have omitted none which have a bearing on our final conclusions. The only ones omitted are those which are so repetitious of others we do include that they would serve no purpose save ennui. As said above, the names are fictitious; the people and their experiences are real.

CHAPTER FOUR

HOME MADE

Modern psychology has given new meaning and great emphasis to the old saying that as the twig is bent, so the tree inclines. The fact is not very new. The Jesuits used to say hundreds of years ago that if they could have a child until he was seven, they cared not who got him later; his faith would be secure. But what is new is the discovery that quite unconscious and completely forgotten influences are as important as conscious training. Therefore, a step toward an understanding of how Communists are made should take us into their homes.

When we get there, we find that outwardly they are much like the homes of anybody else, except that there are perhaps more comforts and educational opportunities than the average. The relationships within those homes are not outwardly unusual either, but we seem to note the presence of a greater than average rigidity of discipline or a more than unusually dominant parent. These things make for rebellion on the part of a certain type of child.

The facts are clear in the stories which former Communists write to explain their entire careers. Here is the account of Harry, the writer, who has become an ardent anti-Communist but without bitterness. He is older than most of our subjects, was in the party longer, and (doubtless because of his profession) expresses himself rather more forcefully and clearly. He writes:

"I joined the Communist party in 1927 at the age of 32. But I had been a close sympathizer ever since 1917. Previously I had been a Socialist and a pacifist.

"I was born into an upper-middle-class family in Southern California. I was a rebel against parental authority in very early boyhood, and left home against my parents' wishes to attend art school at 15. From then on, I was independent of my parents, financially and spiritually.

"At the age of 12 I read the Rubáiyát, Ingersoll, Paine, and became an atheist. At 13 I listened to a street-corner talk by a Socialist named Kilpatrick on 'War—What For' and was deeply affected by two ideals: the abolition of war, and the concept of a cooperative commonwealth in which service would replace the profit motive. Since in the suburb where I lived my boyhood, and in California generally, there was little real poverty, as compared with what I have seen since, the economic consideration played only a minor role.

"Socialism opened up a new world to my imagination. I had been in rebellion against the dull, plodding, materialistic, petty-bourgeois life of a small town, and the equally uninteresting life of Los Angeles where I attended art school. All of the interesting people I met were artists, writers, and other intellectuals, almost all of whom were Socialists and pacifists. (This, of course, was before World War I.) In contrast to my conservative, Republican father, a businessman who was a frustrated intellectual from Maine with a long line of Puritan ancestors, many of whom were ministers, these new friends seemed wonderful. Through my contact with local Socialists, I met Socialists from New York and all over the country, including Eugene V. Debs, Albert Rhys Williams, Walter Packard, Jack London, J. Stitt Wilson, Job Harriman, etc. This was thrilling and flattering.

"These were the years of utopian socialism. I began to read Marx and gradually became a 'scientific Socialist'—sure of all the answers to every social problem. This gave me a feeling of superiority and made me feel part of a great, world-wide movement that eventually would win and save mankind from every evil.

"With this idealistic background, the Russian Revolution came in 1917. I was then teaching school. When the Bolsheviks won over the Mensheviks, I sympathized with the Bolsheviks because I felt that the moderate Socialists were weak, lacked courage and decisiveness, did not dare carry out the Socialist program of nationalization of the means of production, and in addition the Socialists supported 'imperialist' war while the Communists were against war.

"I married, when 19 years of age, a girl who was sympathetic to my views, but much less revolutionary than I. Her influence was always on the cautious side, especially after we had two children.

"On the advice of Upton Sinclair, one of my early mentors, I enlisted in the Medical Corps in World War I, as a decent compromise between my pacifism and a belief that Imperial Germany was the greater evil. I served in France 13 months. On return I taught at Brookwood Labor College, which Norman Thomas had helped to found. After one year I resigned because I had completely repudiated pacifism and had become more and more sympathetic to communism. Returning to California, I taught until 1924, when I came to New York to work for Amtorg [the Company set up by the Soviet government to handle

United States trade and, as it later appeared, certain phases of espionage] chartering steamships. This coincided with a divorce.

"By 1927 my former wife no longer needed much help in supporting the two children, and I decided to throw myself fully into the Communist movement. At that time Amtorg preferred that their employees who were Americans should not be openly party members, and I saw no reason to join the party until I could go all the way. I resigned from the company and took a job doing publicity for the party and its dual trade unions, at the nominal salary of $40 weekly, of which an average of about $30 was actually paid.

"Meantime I had met a girl at the Passaic strike and married again. We had no children. She left me to marry a Communist after I had dropped out of party activity in 1935.

"I did not break with the party, however, but with Earl Browder's approval retired to the country on the excuse that I wanted to write a book. Then came an opportunity to go to Russia as leader of a tourist party. I had been debating through 1935 and 1936 whether or not to break openly. In this period I read omnivorously the literature of the left and right oppositions—Trotsky, Brandler, Bukharin, Lovestone, *et al.* My inclination was not to resume activity in the party, nor to break openly with it either.

"My observations and experiences in the Soviet Union, and later in Spain during the civil war, persuaded me to make the open break and to denounce Stalinism. But through 1937 to about 1940, I still considered myself a Leninist. By 1943 I had repudiated not only Leninism but Marxism.

"I have traveled quite extensively all over the U.S.A., to England, Scandinavia, Russia, Germany, France, Mexico. I was the third child in a family of four sons. All of my brothers are Republicans and successful professional and businessmen leading what seems to me full lives. All of us did well in school, but my record was, I think, more brilliant. I engaged in high school and college in various sports, and was above average in basketball, boxing, and football. I still enjoy sports.

"The income of my father was, until he went bankrupt due to the inability of orange growers to pay their bills because their oranges were frozen two years running, about $10,000 annually, and after that, $5,000. As a teacher I got about $3,000. As an employee of Amtorg, $4,000. As a Communist functionary—mostly editing and publicity— about $2,000. During the period of party membership, I interrupted my service to the cause to increase my income when my wife was sick and debts had accumulated, and earned $7,000 in one year. My salary now (1951)) is $7,800.

"I would add that all of my experience and knowledge of Communists personally, and I know most of the top and middle echelons quite well, bears out the theory that Communists seldom or never join the movement under the illusion that it will increase their incomes. Most of the Communists I have known were capable of earning from two to ten times as much as they were paid by the party, in other occupations. The psychological motive, not the economic, is predominant. After all, they are not idiots. This is likewise true of rank-and-file workers. They risk losing their jobs by party membership, and they give up chances of becoming trade-union officials.

"I would say that I am more successful professionally as a result of my Communist experience because of the nature of my occupation—writing and editing. The experience I gained qualified me for the jobs I have held since I broke. That is likewise true of many if not most ex-Communists. While some have suffered from hysterical anti-communism as exemplified by McCarthyism, this is not true of the majority. Today you will find ex-Communists in the leadership of AF of L and CIO unions, in government service, in teaching, and in every other profession where knowledge of communism is an asset.

"However, this must be qualified by this observation: in the immediate months and even years after one breaks from the Communist party, there is usually loneliness, insecurity, and often difficulty in finding a job. Fear of these things often deters Communists from quitting the party, especially those who are older. You lose your friends, your faith, your sense of security and importance. I was fortunate in having friends who repudiated Stalinism in the same period. Even so, it was a terrible, heart-breaking experience for a while. After devoting years of your life, enduring deprivations, for a cause, it is hard to admit you have been foolish, that you have helped build up a Frankenstein monster threatening every ideal for which you have made sacrifices; it is hard to repudiate part of yourself.

"I would quickly add, however, a warning that the sacrifices made by the Communist, especially in the economic sense and even those who go to jail for the cause, can easily be overemphasized. Like most other Communists, 'the good life' to me was not one of comfort and luxury. If I had to eat hamburger and beans rather than lobster and steak, if I had to live in an East Side railroad flat inhabited by bedbugs, if I could not go to the theater as often as I might wish, if I had to buy my clothes at Crawfords rather than Brooks Brothers, I did not particularly mind. The compensations were 'spiritual' and comparable in a sense to those felt by dedicated souls in the service of a religion, particularly Catholics. I went in 1930 from a $7,000-a-year job back to a CP post at less than half that without any great feeling of hardship or suffering.

"International events rather than domestic affairs played the decisive role in my decision to quit the CP, and I think you will find that this is true of almost all ex-Communists. The degeneration of the Soviet bureaucracy, the rise of Russian nationalism and repudiation of internationalism, the purge of the comrades of Lenin in 1934-1935 and particularly in 1936-1938, the treacherous role of the Comintern in the Spanish Civil War, in short, the liquidation of all the idealism to which the earlier Bolsheviks gave at least lip-service, has been the major factor. Later with many who still deceived themselves even after the purge, etc., it was the Stalin-Hitler pact, or the suppression of Jewish life in the USSR, or the aggressive imperialism of the Stalinists, or the attempt to put all artists, writers, scientists, in uniform, not only in Moscow but in Hollywood—or some other of the various and multitudinous aspects of totalitarianism such as slave labor—that induced individuals to leave the CP.

"Here again I would like to enter a word of warning: those who were never Communists are inclined to condemn ex-Communists whenever they quit the party; those who left early are inclined to be intolerant of those who left later. I have been asked by exiled Mensheviks: how could you remain a Communist after the persecution of Democratic Socialists which began as early as 1923? The trials of the Mensheviks and Social Revolutionists and Anarchists in those years foreshadowed the purges of 1936-1938. And others who quit in 1936 say that anyone who could stomach the purges then, and the starvation of millions in the collectivization of farms earlier, and the other numerous atrocities committed by the Bolsheviks, must be completely lost, corrupted, degenerated. And then there are those who remained CP members until the Stalin-Hitler pact, who argue that after that final betrayal of Communist idealism, no one could possibly be a Communist for reasons that can be respected.

"My reply is that any such thinking is false; if a person joined the party yesterday and quits tomorrow, or next year, his case should be examined on its individual merits. He may have been just as sincere as I was, or any other ex-Communist. Budd Schulberg and Frank Tuttle [two of the movie crowd who got over being Communists] seem to be instances of this truth. Even today, communism has its appeal, and those deceived should not be condemned to the outer darkness, but won over, and when genuinely disillusioned, accepted in decent society.

"I was rather attracted by the secrecy of the CP, while simultaneously rejecting any concealment of my own view. At one time, I considered that secrecy was necessary, especially in nondemocratic countries. Cloak-and-dagger methods, espionage in a 'good' cause, have a romantic appeal unquestionably, not only for Communists but generally. Today, the underground movements in the Iron Curtain countries have that kind of appeal.

"As a child I found it hard to make friends. As a Socialist and later as a Communist, and today as an anti-Communist, I experience no such difficulty. But the key fact is that socialism and communism did overcome that difficulty. I met congenial souls.

"I quit the party quietly without any public declaration at the end of 1935. It was not until 1937 that I wrote an article attacking Stalinism in Spain. The occasion was the 'May Day uprising' in Barcelona, which I had previously been told by George Mink, an NKVD agent, would be engineered by the Communists to end the control of Catalonia by the POUM and CNT [the two big labor organizations of Republican Spain]. I was so outraged by this, on top of the treacherous role of Stalinists in Spain, that I could not justify to my conscience my previous policy of 'above the battle' neutrality in the struggle between various factions in the Socialist and Communist movements.

"In the first years after I left, I refused to give any testimony to the FBI or other government agencies; I abhorred the role of informer. Today, I consider the Stalinists worse than the Fascists, and am glad to give the FBI any information I may have that may be useful in combating this menace to democracy. But I have refused to become a 'professional witness' in court hearings."

Harry, who does not think much of the Oedipus approach to the motivation of Communists, understands very well, however, that his attitude toward his father and his family had a great deal to do with his later life. He is frank enough to recall a friendless childhood. Obviously the reason is within his personality, since all his brothers reacted quite differently.

In the case of Agnes there is no such understanding of self. Agnes is in her early twenties, a plain, dark, scared, young woman who spent two years in the party and was disillusioned in 1951. She joined, as she left, out of misery; she was a lonely, unhappy, rejected girl. She has earned her own living at clerical jobs for seven years. She begins her story:

"My mother and father were separated for many years. When I was about seven years old my father left my mother with seven children. I was the youngest of them all. My mother preached about how horrible my father was from morning till night. She was a nagging woman."

Whether talking or writing, Agnes came back to her family experiences. She felt both neglected by her older brothers and sisters and resentful of her mother, although the poor woman had been dead for a good many years. It was easy to see that after the misery of her family relationships any other that recognized her as a person would be attractive. She found such relationships in the Communist party.

In between Harry and Agnes, we should rate the experience of Francis Mac—, who writes from the security of a good job and a happy home of the background that led him into the Communist party in the late 1930's:

"I wish I could really help you, because by helping you I would give aid to thousands of young people who suffered as I did—suffered in that period of *release* from a dedication to communism. There is no pain in joining; the pain comes only in the return to decent society. Does not most human pain accompany admission of error?

"I can't believe my background is unique. A loving father who wanted to give me every advantage of education and culture. A mother devout to her church—the Roman Catholic Church. In fact the church was her life and it was nip and tuck for a long time if my younger and only sister would not go into a convent. I dare say my quiet sacrificial mother never was sexually aroused by my father or any other man. Marriage was a duty; children were a duty; in truth, as she would say so often to my then mousy, scared sister, what is life but a duty? It's no sin to be a reactionary Republican in the U.S.A., but a reactionary parent probably never knows that he is 're-acting' to all progress, to all things new and young—including, and maybe particularly, his own children.

"My father inherited some wealth, increased it substantially, lost his increase in the Herbert Hoover apple-selling days, and then made it and more back in the late thirties. I grew up in the late twenties and early thirties. School and college were not difficult to handle. Unlike most party members, I had no obvious infirmities or social disabilities. Yet people were not easy to meet. Friends—or what I thought to be friends—came not quickly, but surely in the end. At least it was so with boy friends. My sister was my only girl friend for many years. She needed me, and I enjoyed what I could do to help her fend off Mother. I guess she also helped me stand up to Papa, but then she could handle the old man, even though she was three years younger than I.

"Our home was happy as homes go—you know, contented, and peaceful. But Pop worked late every evening, spent three nights a week out at work or the club, and really hated to take vacations. He would ship us off with Mother. Pop was generous in all attitudes except toward political economy and politics. I guess he was afraid of changes. He had suffered in the Hoover change. He was a routine type. He was generous with gifts and free with money to a fault. I don't know when I started to buck him—but soon I was arguing with him on every item in the morning N. Y. *Times* which he read word for word and agreed with to the point of my quiet exasperation. One of my earliest big tiffs was about the Doheny and Sinclair theft of the oil reserves of the nation, and Pop defended the *Times'* silence or worse on the early La Follette accusations. I didn't know any of the facts and now only know that I was for La Follette and against Pop. I now realize it could have been any issue, and any La Follette, and still that's not quite the case.

"I had one teacher who opened up to me the great fun of curiosity and the joys of inquiry. This teacher was excited about tenement house legislation, minimum wage laws, and reduced tariffs. He probably never went further in his own political thinking, but he got us kids into real arguments, without name-calling and without any feeling of defeat if one changed one's ideas. This last, I think, was what irritated Pop most. I wouldn't get mad at him, at least outwardly, and he couldn't make me change my mind just because he disagreed. If I did change my mind, he would rub it in, and try to make me feel ashamed. On this score he always lost out.

"How does this tie in with my membership in the Communist party? I don't exactly know, except that when I got out I became close and friendly first of all with my father. He then had enough sense not to rub it in, even though he had been ashamed of me, even more than if I had had syphilis or robbed his bank.

"Few people get out of the party because of facts. If the reasons stated are factual, such as the Communist Korean attack, or the Stalin-Hitler pact, or the Stalin purges, I suggest you look deeper. For then you will find many hard facts of greater power admittedly have been unmeasured and unappraised by them in the past, long before the moment of withdrawal.

"Fact tells you that very few Americans join the Communist party and that this means the movement does not fit into our pattern of culture. But Lenin tells you: don't worry about numbers, this is a movement of the elite, the rich, and the brainy.

"In fact you know that your own father confused your acts of defiance with acts of youthful growing up, although he should have known that the purpose of all education is that children should cut those iron umbilical cords. But in the party, the father is not as loving and tolerant as your own father and still you make no contest. This is a father of your own choice and if he is wrong, you were wrong in choosing him. Hence, you forgive your newly selected father—or rather rationalize your disagreement into a kind of self-hypnotic submissiveness.

"One foreign ex-priest in the party was the only person I met who fully understood what discipline and the need for discipline meant to the members. It isn't quite masochism, because together with the joy of suffering, there is the sadistic joy of spying and telling on everyone else. The hunt for deviation is not too unlike the old inquisitions in the churches—even though the point of the Marxist pin seems to be big enough for only one angel at one time.

"Not until I got out of the party did I become an equal of my old man. Then I understood him and liked him. I'm sorry he died so soon after we knew each other. I'll always remember that I could say to him:

" 'Dad, remember you once said to me, "You think too much"? I hated you for that but I was helped back to you in an odd, perverse way when some of those chattering unexciting people who make up the CP, people who accept without tremor great dangers, said to me, "You think too much." ' "

These three represent widely separated groups in our society. But they are typical of many ex-Communists.

Through a great many of the other stories there are scattered such comments as these:

"Mine was a typical struggle of an adolescent against authority, of a first-generation American against immigrant parents' ways."

"I was ashamed of my parents and fought to disassociate myself from them."

"My father was a strict disciplinarian and wanted his children, at least his son, to follow his pattern of living."

"Discipline in our family was strict and I was outspokenly rebellious on this score."

And there are some unconscious admissions of chafing at family restraints, evidenced in such comments as:

"I was in an intellectual revolt, not so much against my parents as the mores and ideas they shared with the majority of the population."

Of course this hostility to parents or rejection by parents happens to a great many more Americans than become Communists. But one thing seems to be true about all the cases we have cited, and a great many more who closely resemble them in this feature of the family background. While they rebelled or were hurt, they still wanted a father upon whom to lean, from whom to take direction, and a mother to comfort and love them. Some people of this kind embrace an authoritarian religion. Some marry a person who resembles the parent they secretly want. And some become Communists. It is not without significance that so many members of the party refer to "Papa" Stalin where the rest of their compatriots would call him "Uncle Joe."

Almost as frequently as we find divorces and suicides in the family backgrounds of Communists, we find the members orphaned at a relatively early age. Even oftener we find the child's individuality destroyed by living parents.

Especially in one to whom love was denied, the party finds an individual ripe for a final break with the family and all that the family stood for. And it seems to be true that once family loyalty has been broken down, the collapse of loyalty to another group, whether union or civic organization or the country itself, is easier too.

As the careers of former Communists are analyzed, it is apparent that they are not recruited from the juvenile delinquent or the player of hookey on the one hand or from the passively obedient children on the other. The good boy and girl, who studied hard and attended school faithfully but were the family rebels against domineering parents, make the reliable party members, as they usually make reliable members of any group to whom they give allegiance. It is not only this trait that leads them to communism, but this combined with others.

It would appear that the rebel's desire for a papa adds to the pain of his break with the party. It seems to the disillusioned member as tragic as if he had discovered that an adored parent was unworthy—a crook or a hypocrite. The former Communist can seldom turn again to his real parents. Many among our collaborators sought a substitute in a dominant friend or spouse or colleague, or in a job with a paternalistic organization, or—in some cases—in a church.

Whether tied too long to their parents or abandoned too soon by their parents, children have a natural inclination to attempt some sort of defiance, a sort of declaration of their own independence. For some it may be a secret declaration, and if they join the Communist party, it is frequently a secret but nonetheless cherished defiance.

The relations of the Communist to brothers and sisters are often as interesting and perhaps as revealing as his attitude toward parents. We noted, for example, that very often if one of two brothers goes Communist, the other is likely to be conservative. But if an older brother goes Communist, his younger sister seems likely to follow him, or a younger brother may follow the older sister. When brothers do find themselves together in the party, their relations are such that one former Communist who was being psychoanalyzed was told by the analyst:

"If you had not gotten out, your brother would have."

Perhaps the story of the D—s, brother Herbert and sister Anne, as told by him, will illustrate the family experience of many. He writes:

"I came from a family which has been in the upper middle class. As a matter of fact, the family is just about getting into the top group in the United States in dollar terms. My mother was married late in life, and there were two children, my sister, Anne, and myself. I went to private schools and one of the top colleges. I took dancing lessons and music lessons and the trip to Europe usual for children of the rich.

"My father had extreme work habits and as far back as I remember wanted me to take over his investment business. I was a quiet kid and not too well coordinated physically. I had only one real intimate friend in my youth, and that was my sister, who was younger and who also went to good schools and colleges. She was very good looking, and I grew up convinced that I was ugly.

"While at college I decided to become a lawyer. Before finishing the law course, I found I was equipped neither for courtroom acting nor for transmitting confidence to clients in an office. But I did get interested in labor unions and the problems of discrimination. Through others who felt as I did, especially the girl I later married, I joined the party. There was no break from my home. As a matter of fact, I had started to feel secure in my relation to my father. I made up my mind I would not go into his business and had the nerve to tell him so. My mother was a frightful Roosevelt-hater and although my father voted Republican all his life, deep down he realized that Roosevelt probably saved our economic system.

"My sister, a couple of years after I joined, also joined. Amusingly enough, she had fallen in love with a member of the young Communist movement.

"My wife, my sister, and I had several rich years of interrelationship, discussing social problems and feeling effective doing little chores which the party gives to its young members. You will never know the feeling of dedication that comes even from painting signs for picket lines or distributing pamphlets.

"Of course our parents did not know that we had joined the Communist party, and they still don't know even though they thought we were very far left and nutty. We kept up a personal relationship of a sort with our parents and felt that deep down they rather envied us our enthusiasms.

"People don't leave the Communist party at one determined moment. It is a gradual process of being reconverted to democracy. It so happened that our reconversion occurred at the time of the Stalin-Hitler pact. The somersault in thinking we could no longer manage.

"It is my best guess that hundreds of Communists would leave the party except for one reason: They are afraid of being smeared in the press. They are afraid to tell their parents, to whom they have so often lied on the subject in the past. They are afraid to tell their friends, whom they have fooled in the past. Above all, they are afraid they can never get a job, and the fight for existence is not to be sneezed at. Some of our ex-Communist friends were discussing the other evening the possibility of making a study as to just what has been done in the United States to get jobs for former embezzlers, burglars—and Communists. It still seems that being a Communist at *any* time in life is the one irreparable sin. Some day this country must grow up so that ex-Communists are treated with at least as much fairness as ex-Klansmen, those bigots who in their attitude toward humanity and society are infinitely worse than Communists."

Herbert reveals one trait which is common to many of those who told us of their experience—and to a lot of other people, too. He thinks everybody else in the party was like himself, that they lied to their parents and were afraid to tell their friends what they were doing. Actually, a good many were proud of their membership, proud of their "sacrifice," proud of their advanced thinking, and so on.

The sort of family background which all of these former Communists from well-to-do, well-educated families reveal is a very different one from the minority who were, so to speak, born into the party, who became Communists as naturally as a Lowell or a Cabot goes to Harvard. These latter are trained consciously for a role in the party, whereas the others are the result of largely unconscious or subconscious attitudes on the part of their parents. Both groups have this in common: they experienced a lack of affectionate intimacy in the home.

The Communist parent is not supposed to have too much time for mere children; the party and its work absorbs him if he is a faithful member, to the exclusion of domestic ties. Children are carefully trained in Communist ideology and insulated from other influences. The parents are not without tenderness for the children, but they are as rigid in their discipline as any reactionary tyrant. The difference is that they know just what they are doing when they coerce the child, while the reactionary parent is doing it unwittingly and therefore with very different results. Communist coercion has a purpose and a design.

Stephen Z., for example, was the youngest of seven children of a foreign-born, very poor couple who worked in the textile mills of a small Eastern city. The sons and daughters all went to work when they finished grammar school, but Stephen later attended a labor college. His mother remained a professing Catholic until her husband died, and her open break with the Church coincided with Stephen's entry into the party, a situation which may bespeak more than pure coincidence.

"I grew up with the party," he explains. "Most of the family were members. I was very active, especially in the youth movements. We never kept the fact of our membership secret; we were quite proud of the fact. Remember we were going to make a 'decent' world. While a good disciplined member of the party, I felt every word, decision, and act was the gospel truth."

While still a young man, Stephen fell in love with a girl who was not a member of the party. Just meeting people who were outside the influence of communism led him to see the world with new eyes. A friendly, outgiving person by nature, he listened as well as talked, but he did not communicate his growing doubts to his family, nor has he yet. It took him two years to withdraw quietly from party work after he had made up his mind finally to do so.

"The Stalin-Hitler pact killed any sentiment I may have had left for the party," he says.

By that time he was married and had a small daughter. He became a Socialist, and later joined the Lovestone group because his basic beliefs had not changed very much. Looking back at it, he thinks his party training was of value.

"It taught me unselfishness and self-sacrifice and tolerance," he explains.

But, he adds, he has discovered the pleasure of thinking for himself, of making his own decisions as to what is good and bad in world affairs without taking his opinions ready-made.

At 37, Joseph G. has been out of the party for a dozen years, but he is still seeking for a substitute. He too was brought up in the party in a middle-sized industrial city with a large foreign-born population. As he tells it:

"I was born in 1915 of parents who had been in the Jewish Bund in Poland and were Socialists in this country. My aunts, uncles, older cousins, and close friends of the family were also involved in the Socialist movement.

"My father died in 1919 of the flu. My mother became a Communist during the split in the Socialist party. A number of aunts and uncles and close family friends also either joined or were influenced by the Bolshevik revolution. In some cases either the aunt or the uncle were *left* and the other *right*. Other than my mother, of those I loved the most, my favorite aunt, sister to my deceased father, went into the Communist movement. Her husband, by the way, remained a stanch Social Democrat—in fact, probably the leading Social Democrat in our city.

"I was sent to Pioneer Camp, a children's camp [for the young of the party], and was completely indoctrinated into the Communist movement in this country. Handed out leaflets in front of factories, etc., at the age of ten. Went to classes where I was taught American history from a revolutionary Marxist viewpoint—was told the story of the Astors, Morgans, Rockefellers, etc., in those early years. I was so completely indoctrinated that I didn't learn that others than Communists or Socialists had anything to do with the labor movement in this or any other country until I was about 15 or 16.

"I heard discussions and witnessed a few family break-ups because of the Troskyite and then the Lovestoneite splits in the CP. These troubled me greatly for obvious reasons; family friends today were not tomorrow.

"At 16 I developed a strong friendship for a boy of the same age whose parents were Lovestoneites. This boy and his parents and their family friends had influence upon me, but not enough to lead me to break from my CP beliefs, though from 1931 to 1934 I was more or less neutralized.

At that point I became an active young Communist, did some organization work in the South and then in a Communist-dominated union.

"In 1936 I had the belief that all left-wing splinter groups would join the CP, but the beginning of the purge trials of leading Bolsheviks turned my puzzlement over Stalin's actions into hatred. I believed he would be deposed. I went to Spain in December, 1936, as a member of the International Brigade.

"Before I went, I had long discussions with my Lovestoneite friend and had gained sympathy for the POUM. [This was one of the chief labor organizations and non-Communist.] In Spain I kept my mouth shut and ears open; I had already learned that free discussion was dead in Communist movements, and that if one attempted it, one was dead too! In Spain I saw with my own eyes the complete betrayal of revolutionary Marxism by Stalinism, as well as the breakdown of libertarian thought and behavior. Yet—yet I also saw the Communist youth of the world in its most energetic and heroic role. The emotional internal struggle against reason was *almost* overpowering. It left me practically in a state of numbness—the hell with thinking about it—I'll just roll along.

"I was almost mortally wounded in March of 1937 at the Madrid-Jarama front. I recovered and convalesced in Murcia. I was repatriated in the fall of 1937, but not before having a close call with the chief of police of the Brigade, who was asked to look after me in a 'fatherly' way by a compatriot of his, a nurse with whom I was very friendly.

"Back in the U.S., I was medically as well as financially taken care of by the Friends of the Abraham Lincoln Brigade. Then I was given a job in a completely Communist-controlled union in New York City. I went to a few meetings of the party and then stopped going completely. My job was purely secretarial, but I was asked a number of times to do organizational work, which I refused on grounds of physical disability.

"In the meantime I started going to symposiums and lectures by the Lovestoneites, Trotskyites, and Socialists. This was reported to my superiors by people who saw me at these functions and I was called in a few times to answer questions of why and how come. I stood on my democratic rights or just shrugged. At the beginning these interviews were on a very friendly, father-son basis. Later, after the Stalin-Hitler pact, I was told either it stops or I go. Finally in November, 1939, I was told that my employment was terminated. I caused them some embarrassment by picketing as a victim of the Stalin-Hitler pact and passing out leaflets which summarized my story.

"For at least a year previously I had attended meetings of the Independent Labor League of America (Lovestoneite) and upon the termination of my job and connection with the Communist party I became an active member of the ILLA until its demise.

"My withdrawal from the party had taken in reality two years. In that interval I had slowly given up my party friendships except for two or three very close ones. At the final parting, these two or three gave me up. One, a close friend whom I had acquired in Spain, said, 'You know, J.G., if you're a Trotskyite, I can't be friends with you.' That was the end of that, though I loved him dearly. Later he lost his life on the Murmansk run, a life which he had been endeavoring to throw away for four or five years.

"Having finally left the Communist movement, I found that I had left a confined, bigoted community. It has taken me since then to *unlearn* how to read, to think, to discuss, to listen—in essence, to learn how to become a member of our relatively free society. It took me ten years to be able to pick up and read *The New Leader* without feeling a sense of guilt. I still haven't unlearned the thought that I have *all* the answers to *all* the ills of our society—of the *whole* world!

"I find I am an emotional anti-Communist in speech, in discussion—a rational anti-Communist in reading, interpreting, and trying to understand the world I—we—live in.

"At present I belong to no political organization. It is my belief that there is none to which I can belong, with my political beliefs, which are still Marxian to a limited extent, though perhaps the real reason is that I am still searching for the absolute party to which I can give absolute devotion. I hope not."

Joseph, and others like him, explain in part why labor has raised up some if not most of our really effective opponents of communism. These workers, although certainly enjoying less economic security than the general run of professionals and business people, are not so dependent emotionally. They can cut themselves off from the party without being so afraid of losing a job or not getting another.

Perhaps this is linked to the lesser hostility to a dominating parent and to a tougher family training. For when father hostility does develop in a left-wing family, it does not seem to be much different than in a family of any other persuasion. This is evidenced in a few remarks by a man who may be called Gerald F., a recruit to the early Communist party from the old American radical organization of "Wobblies"—the Industrial Workers of the World. This man, now elderly, recalls:

"My father was a Socialist. As a son, I fought him. I was very religious. One year the leader of the church ran for governor in my state on the Socialist ticket. My father had suggested that the Socialist candidate be allowed to speak in the church. I fought my father."

Gerald's first reaction to his father's socialism was a deep religious devotion, but when that failed to satisfy him he joined the IWW. It would appear that only a hair separated him at the crucial moment from the crossroads that would have led him to conservatism rather than radicalism.

It seems evident among all those who reacted against their family environment that this environment contributed largely to making them extremists. They could accept nothing less than an absolute, and the Communist party is one of the few organizations in this country that pretends to have absolute answers. The boy or girl who is brought up to regard every problem subject to a completely right-wrong solution is already on the road to communism or some other extremist "ism." The child may never get there but is ripe for the plucking.

This in itself may explain why so many Communists in this country are from relatively well-to-do backgrounds. This so-called middle class is more likely to indulge in illusions of absolute rightness and wrongness in politics, education, and economics as well as in religion and morals. To the rebels against parental views who yet accept the validity of the basic premise that absolute solutions are attainable, the Communist party makes a strong appeal. That, in turn, is more likely to attract the educated and relatively prosperous than the manual worker.

When all this is said, it must be admitted that although we have probably interviewed more former Communists than anyone else in this country, we have not obtained dogmatic answers to questions we have raised. Of course there is no one typical home for developing Communists any more than there is for members of the Elks, Lions, or

American Civil Liberties Union. But on the basis of our material, we could advance a few tentative conclusions. Or rather, if one of the Congressional committees busily chasing names would spend a little of its money to produce just one report on why American youths join the Communist movement, we think the section on family background probably would show:

That the parents are sober, ambitious, and industrious with a genuine but perhaps not very intelligent concern for the education and prosperity of their children. Few of the homes ever experienced real want; much more often provision was made for higher education.

That the parents are far from ungodly and the homes are well versed in formal religion.

That the parents tend to be book-readers rather than television-viewers or "comic"-strip addicts. They would be more likely to subscribe to the New York *Times, Herald Tribune, Christian Science Monitor,* or Louisville *Courier-Journal* than the *Daily News,* Chicago *Tribune,* or Hearst press. This preference is an indication of their cultural level, not of agreement or disagreement with the editorial position of these papers. We do not think the editorial position of the press has much influence either for good or bad these days.

That, when a Communist son is obviously hostile to his father, that parent was more active in the Chamber of Commerce, Union League, taxpayers' association, and the like than in charities or liberal organizations. Papa is usually a stout fellow, often outspoken in defense of his belief in capitalism which did so well for him, and displaying little imagination as to the fate or the character of people less fortunate. If he was a manufacturer, he was probably patronizing toward his help but definitely anti-union.

That the homes were not without cultural interests, especially music and the arts. If the head of the house was a worker, he was generally skilled, above the average intellectually, and active in trade unions or benevolent societies.

That if Papa was the Caspar Milquetoast of the family, Mama was a rather overwhelming character—this of families not broken by divorce or death or desertion as so many are. In any case, it would appear that the parents were not truly partners in a marriage. Either one is dominant or there is bickering and quarreling or indifference and distaste.

We think the study of the children would show, as our own has indicated, the following:

That they experienced a great deal of fear in the home, particularly in the home of an intellectual, a professional, or a businessman. This fear led to secrecy, to concealment, or to excessive rebelliousness, a sort of overfighting of the parents' point of view. The children preferred to talk things over with their friends whenever they could not do so frankly with their parents, and this prepared them for the secrecy of an underground party.

That the children were ashamed of parents of foreign birth, ashamed that Father had a beard or Mother an accent and wore a shawl.

That many of the children grew up with an inner craving for discipline, for an authority. They could not accept their father as authority, but they needed someone. Many of our older ex-Communists drifted first into socialism, but there was not enough discipline for them. The late Heywood Broun, looking for certainty, became a Socialist, but soon left. He very nearly joined the Communist party, being deterred at the last moment by the stealth and dishonesty of the party aims and leadership. Instead he joined the Catholic Church. In much the same way, a good many Communists were brought up in devout homes but turned from the certainty of their father's faith to that of the new Soviet "religion."

That children are seldom influenced by teachers in joining the Communist party. This seems to tie in with the ineffectiveness of books and speeches as recruiting agents.

In short, we think that the study we hope might be made would show that Communists are partly made in the home. But only partly. Many children with the same family background or even the same families are not attracted to communism at all. Obviously, the study would show other influences, too. And it would show why they are important.

~~~~~~~~~~~~~~~~~~~~~~~~~~~~~~

CHAPTER FIVE

YOUTHFUL ERRORS

THE fact that so many youngsters join the Communist party or the Young Communist League in their teens is related to family background and attitudes. So is the fact that many of them leave in two or three years or less. If the parents have to take the blame for the joining, they might get the credit for the leaving, too.

These youngsters are the Communists who are potentially the most valuable to society. They are earnest, hard-working, studious youths, generally passionate for justice. They come mostly from good homes of American citizens. If they also are handicapped by shyness, ugliness, an unfortunate social background (from their own point of view), and inner dreams of power or delights in secrecy, they still can be useful citizens. In other words, their advantages seem to be greater than their defects.

From the number of young people who have told us of how they entered the party at high school age and left in or before their early twenties, it would appear that communism could be deprived of its chief recruiting ground, youth, by an intelligent social approach. The indiscriminate branding of all ex-Communists as irredeemable, the obstacles put in the way of those who quit, tend to freeze these youngsters in the party. Even when the finger was pointed less accusingly than it has been in the last few years, many disillusioned youths were afraid to quit the party. They were afraid of what their comrades might do. When to that is added the fear of what the rest of the community might do, it is small wonder that they feel paralyzed, unable to move.

It has always been natural for the young to be radical; at times the conservative youth has been an object of suspicion. When radicalism goes so far as to lead a boy or girl into the Communist party, all the circumstances should be considered before a judgment which will blight a life is passed. It must be remembered that while adult, informed citizens may know that the party is the agent of a foreign system, the very extravagance of the McCarthys of this world can bewilder youth. If some greatly admired figures are denounced as Communists, it is quite natural for a young person to think that communism may not be so bad, that the Communists are right in talking of persecution and lies. When an organization of supposedly intelligent businessmen like the National Association of Manufacturers says that certain social reforms of which most decent people think highly are Communist, why should a student not admire communism? When an organization of supposedly intelligent professional men like the American Medical Association says health insurance is Communist, why should a bright youth not go along with communism? If Mrs. Roosevelt is a sympathizer of communism, as some antagonistic people say untruthfully, a youngster who properly admires Mrs. Roosevelt may sympathize, too. Former Communists well understand the value to the party of the wild, blanket allegations made by the McCarthys and the bigots of the right. Above all youth with vitality, though short on wisdom, is not deterred from joining by smears directed at those who leave. Youth is reluctant to believe their sins and errors are without redemption.

There are, of course, other reasons which attract a certain kind of idealist to the Communist party. Some of these reasons are the same ones that tend to get him out fairly soon; others pull in the opposite direction. The personal tragedy of many of these youngsters is in the pull and haul of these conflicting motives.

Most of those we have seen or heard from, but not all, have had a succession of disappointments in their families. They have not had sympathetic parents or have had no parents at all; nearly half of them (although we think this is far higher than the party average) have been children of broken homes, divorce, or separation. Others were orphaned at an early age or lost one parent. Some of these and many of the others have been overshadowed in the family by brothers or sisters or both. They have been lonely children very often, and the Communist youth movement gave them a sense of belonging, an illusion of popularity that marked the high point of their lives. As might be expected of children with this background and temperament, they were not attracted by competitive athletics even in those cases where they were fairly good at sports.

Consider the case of Betty R—, youngest of three daughters born to an immigrant German father who had followed the pattern of the American success story so closely that by the time Betty was a little girl he had a business which brought him an income of about $25,000 a year. He had adapted himself admirably to American business practices, but not so well to American social habits, especially in the family. His wife, also German-born, shared his ideas of the place of girls in the scheme of things. At least their daughter never could detect any signs of disagreement. Betty, even more than her older sisters, resented this attitude and felt that submission to parental authority would lessen her in the eyes of her school fellows.

Her older sisters were outstanding students in the schools to which she followed them, she recalls, and she worked hard to live up to their records. Also she was an exception to the general lack of interest in sports, for she competed eagerly in school athletics, again seeking approval of her fellows.

Betty entered a coeducational college when she was 17. She was attracted immediately to the group of campus radicals. They seemed to her to be "her kind," for they were contemptuous of parental dogma. Her own father was a liberal in political if not domestic thinking, but she hardly thought his ideas were up to those of her new friends.

When she first began to speak about the reasons why she joined the Young Communist League so promptly after entering college, Betty listed these:

"First, rebellion against authority; second, idealism, a desire to better working conditions, race equality, etc.; third, a desire for social approval from the radical group."

But as she went on talking, she remembered that love was not entirely absent. "My first romance was with a Communist," she said.

She made no secret of her Communist affiliation, and that still further strained her relations with her parents, for her father was bitterly anti-Communist. But she was incessantly active in party affairs on the campus, and became a leader in them. She picked up a rather precocious knowledge of obscure points of parliamentary procedure and organizational discipline. She also was proud of her ability to run a mimeograph machine, one of the examples of that odd joy which Communists from homes like hers derive from doing something useful with their hands.

Betty had been a good party worker for a little more than a year when she began to cool toward the work.

"The literature is dull, uninspired, and poorly written," she said. "Hearing the stupid remarks of party functionaries was one of my first big disillusionments. But while I had what seemed to be intellectual reasons for leaving, I think now they were mere rationalizations of emotional causes. I think my big experience and chance to profit from a mistake helped to bring maturity."

After three months of wavering, Betty left the party, and did it publicly at a Young Communist League meeting.

William E., superficially very different in character, reveals some fundamental similarities to Betty. The son of a small-town, well-to-do conservative with a family background deep in the roots of the United States, William was educated at private schools and a small, select college. His parents had been divorced when he was a small boy—he was the youngest of three—and his mother had remarried. He saw a good deal of both his parents, and says he did not care much for them. He was an ugly, shy little boy, timid as the result of an accident which left him with a slight limp. He, too, followed older brothers to school and college, but where they had been outstanding figures among their fellows, he was withdrawn and rather inclined to seek his friendships among the quieter, studious boys.

In college several of these went into the Communist party—William thinks they were recruited by a "party scout"—and he went along with them. He was then 19. The secrecy of the little group was one of the main attractions for him, and he enjoyed the feeling of how much his membership in the party would upset his father, had he known about it. Apparently it never occurred to him that he might reveal his secret to any member of his family or friends outside the party.

During his years at college where he took a professional degree and in the first few years of his practice in the world outside college, William was an ardent but small cog in the party machine. He gave a quarter of his income for party work and was as active as possible.

"I was only given small chores," he writes, "all of which were very satisfying. Other groups could take a lesson from CP; they fail to give new members any jobs to do. The experience was of great value to me, for I lived a sacrificial, hazardous life."

His satisfaction, however, began to fade after five years. At 24, William was not so sure of the party aims. He "caught them in too many stupid lies." He was beginning to worry about the security of his job. Also, he had married a girl who was a member of the party, but he is a little vague as to whether his wife was also being disillusioned and helped draw him from the party. After two years of worrying over what would happen, he and two friends who were equally dissatisfied quietly withdrew from the party. They just stopped going to meetings, stopped doing the small chores. This was toward the end of World War II.

The representative of a more recent crop of young Communists is Jerry T—, who was a member of the Young Communist League in high school. Now married, he is working and taking college courses at night in order to fit himself for a better job.

The second of three children, he recalls no special family difficulties, but his adolescence was unhappy. He describes his parents as "lower middle class" and they were unable to afford much in the way of luxuries or educational opportunity. Jerry was indifferent to school, both academically and athletically, as were his brother and sister. But at 16 he discovered the Young Communist League and enjoyed active work which seemed to give him a position of leadership among his fellows.

"Largely people get in for emotional reasons, not intellectual ones," he writes now. "That was not my conviction at the time. But it was a significant experience for the bitter members of my generation—and the more neurotic."

Jerry thinks that as "the natural result of my own development," he began to drift away from the party when he was 18. After six months, he decided that it was no longer the road to progress which he had thought, and he told his friends in the party that he was leaving. His parents, rightists and unhappy about their son's Communist affiliations of which they knew generally, were not told he was cutting the bond.

Isobel M. was less concerned about her family reactions so far as telling them of her Communist leanings was concerned. But she remembers an unhappy childhood largely dominated by shame of her parents. The youngest of four children, with two brothers and a sister, her early childhood was strongly affected by the descent of the family fortunes. Her father, after being in what she calls "the upper middle class," suffered serious reverses and by the time Isobel reached her teens, the family was on relief.

"They had no real political opinions, but were vaguely sympathetic to the left," she says.

"My oldest brother was a child prodigy. I myself was a good athlete but never went out for school teams or that sort of thing. I was interested in the theater. The only drama group in the neighborhood was a Communist one. I became active there at an early age and met my friends there. It was a natural step from that to the Young Communist League.

"One brother, not the prodigy, and my sister were members of the party. No one actually persuaded me to join, but I was aware that my joining would please my sister who in many ways fulfilled a mother's role for me. So at 16, when I was in high school, I joined the YCL.

"I was in the YCL for three years. I was influenced both by speakers and literature. The speeches probably had the greater impact. It was a stirring experience to be part of the cheering mob at the Garden when Earl Browder spoke. There was a great feeling of 'belonging.' I thought the CP was the great hope of the working class.

"The intellectual reason for my leaving was because the YCL's position on the Oxford Pledge (for peace) vacillated as Moscow's position shifted. As an idealist, I had been convinced of the rightness of the pledge; I could not unconvince myself merely by hearing that this was no longer The Line. The immediate incident which precipitated the break was the attempted enforcement of a rule prohibiting members from socializing with Trotskyites, alleged Trotskyites, or alleged enemies of the party. Since these categories included several good friends, my closest one among them, I rebelled.

"I resigned. I was informed that my 'case' was to be tried before the entire membership. I attended the meeting, not because I wanted to fight my expulsion, but to make a public statement of the evils in the YCL which had caused me to resign. My own brother was my chief accuser. Needless to say, I was not given a chance to speak my piece."

These stories of young Communists would fit a great many of the ones we have met, with only insignificant changes in detail. They do not indicate an unforgivable sin. These youngsters are well aware that the Communist party in America follows the Moscow line. They know that the real leadership is directed from Russia. But those who get in and out in their school and college days or just after do not know about, nor do they engage in, espionage and similar activities. In fact, they become disillusioned with the party even more than with its principles when they see its shifts on orders from Moscow. This seems to be as great a factor in their quitting as the process of growing up. Maybe in fact it is the evidence of becoming adult.

The consequences, however, are more serious and lasting than those that pursue the youth of the same age who may have joined a teen-age gang of hoodlums or criminals or sex experimenters. The youthful sinner in other sins can expiate and win absolution. The young Communist, especially if ever he lied about belonging to the party, is cut off from a career in government and subject to many handicaps in other professions. In general, the later lives of our four examples above may be typical.

The first thing that happened to Betty R— after she left the party was that she got married. Although she attaches no significance to a suggestion that her feelings for someone not a party member might have been a factor in her quitting, she was married immediately after her break. She was nineteen, and the marriage lasted a year. She soon remarried, and in four years has had two children.

In her case there was no problem of employment to be faced since she never had nor sought a job. Her relations with her family became a little less strained, and are now quite friendly. But Betty is emphatic about the difficulty of starting a new life outside the party.

"They spread the most vicious stories about me," she said, "and to a young girl just getting married that hurt." But she adds: "Leaving was my first chance to analyze my own motives, and that analysis forced me to take the step no matter what the consequences. It also provided me with political insight, into the Communists and into how a group functions."

Asked if she found it pleasant to make her own decisions after leaving the party, she replied simply: "Of course." To get a short answer from a Communist is not a prevalent pattern of conversation. One of her decisions, however, is not to join any other organization. Betty is one of the former Communists who has been made shy of all organized activity.

No special hardships have hounded William E. since he mustered up courage to join two comrades in quitting the party. As is often the case the people who join one by one leave the party in twos and threes. But he still is afraid his past will catch up with him, and it obviously affects him deeply. He, too, has shrunk from joining any other organization; he is afraid of all of them, he says, adding:

"I am increasingly nonpolitical, except sore at the McCarthys who keep people in the party; I guess I enjoy the dignity of making my own decisions now; there are not so many to make in my nonpolitical world."

Obviously William is glad that he is spared the responsibility of making decisions at all. His personality in this respect did not change. It was not easy for him to make a new life, for that is what he had to do inwardly even if the outward pattern of his existence has changed but little. He writes:

"I spent days worrying how to get out and not have to be a squealer at the FBI. I knew what they [party members] did and got me to do under similar circumstances; in one case I even stole books and examination papers from anti-CP boys at school. I was afraid they would advise my employer of my membership. I was afraid of the Congressional and other investigating committees which smear and keep boys in the party. I'm still in peril. If my company knew it, I'd be fired though I'm not in a security position."

William's fears are much more pressing than Betty's because he had once, pursuant to the party policy of secrecy which he found so attractive at the time, officially denied being a member of the party. He doesn't know how to get out of that one because confession now, he thinks, would be ruinous. He is bitter against the party—"to me the benefits in sacrifice were great but to society the movement is evil," and against the press—"the Press is stupid. It plays the CP game," as well as against the Congressional committees and McCarthy. Behind it all, is the evident fact that the personality which made him a Communist in the course of its development has not changed materially and has not enabled him to be any happier or more useful.

His attitude toward "squealing," a distaste ingrained in most young people of his background, is widespread. While the FBI is not interested in encouraging tale-bearers, it is perhaps natural for former Communists who feel strongly about tattling to include the agency in their derogatory remarks about the "squealer" just as schoolboys dislike a teacher to whom a companion has "squealed."

Jerry T— has not ceased to be a radical just because he left the Communist party. He now belongs to a group with Trotskyite leanings led by former followers of that exiled Bolshevik.

"On leaving the Communist party," says Jerry, "I made full and deliberate disclosure to my friends, told them all, including party members, that I was quitting. I cannot remember that there was any particular effect upon my family relationships.

"But I couldn't get into college then because of my YCL activities in high school peace strikes. I was afraid to apply for any civil service job.

"The historical materialistic orientation had a great effect on me, and it still remains with me. My experience in the Communist party made me fight for the slogans they supported, e.g., the fight against war, but I consider the party a reactionary party now. For me there has not been a great change in my manner of living or my friends, although I live a little better now."

Isobel M. is one of the few who now thinks she derived little benefit from her experience as a Communist.

"I could have spent my time and effort more profitably," she says.

Probably this feeling arises in part from the difficulties she experienced in adjusting to her new life. She explains:

"I lost many of my friends, even though as things turned out most of them quit, too, eventually. I was afraid that my ex-comrades would pass the word on to members or sympathizers in the professional theater, of whom there were many, and that I would not be able to get work. There was a strained relationship between my brother [the one who had been her accuser in the YCL] and me for several years. My sister was living in another city at the time. On her rare visits home, she avoided discussing politics with me.

"But I am rather pleased that I had the courage to leave when I did. It was tough learning to walk without the emotional help of the party. I have no particular fear of the American Communist party; I think it's proven ineffective under fairly favorable conditions. Ordinarily democratic processes are sufficient to keep it in check.

"I felt that I had grown up when I had weathered the break and earned my right to decide things for myself."

Since then Isobel has married; her fears for her career have been absorbed in the preoccupations of motherhood—she has two small children.

These one-time youthful Communists all have been punished, and are still being punished, for their youthful error. The two young women in these particular cases seem to have come off more lightly than the men, largely because they have retired into the relative security of marriage. But neither the boy who denied his membership nor the one who made no secret of it has been able to progress as far as they might have if they never had joined. The one is obviously handicapped by his fears, which are justified, and the other by recognition of the fact that his open avowal of his Communist past and radical present bar certain lines of employment which he would like. Their fate is not encouraging to other youthful Communists who might want to get out.

A great many who have quit the party are barred by hysterical employers and even more live in fear of hysteria. But this is not a necessary feature of our war against communism. There are some encouraging signs amid the gloom spread by the red-baiters and the red informers or the extremists of right and left.

One that seems significant has come from, of all places, the army. Leo Kaye is not one of those who has written his story for us. He is rather a *cause célèbre,* celebrated because in the 1950's our American society acted intelligently in handling a man who had been a Communist in his youth. He even had his case written up in *The Reader's Digest.*

Leo Kaye was born to the party, like several we have mentioned in the previous chapter. His father was a Russian immigrant who was an ardent party man. Leo, born in Brooklyn in 1917, was sent to Communist schools and camps, was an active member of the Young Communist League at 15, and was so busy in his Communist activities that he was expelled from two high schools. He became a copy boy on the *Daily Worker*, started to become a newspaperman, and then began to look at life. He quit the YCL when he was 21 without joining the party, enlisted in the Canadian Army at the beginning of World War II, transferred to the American Army after Pearl Harbor, and served until 1945. He liked the army and re-enlisted in 1947. He fell in love, married, fathered a baby, discovered religion through his wife, was promoted to sergeant, and suddenly on October 4, 1950, was notified that he was dismissed from the army because he had once been a Communist. Leo Kaye borrowed enough money to go to Washington. Not the least of his reasons for being celebrated is that he managed to see a general on his first try. The general put his story before four other generals, and Leo Kaye was permitted to re-enlist without taking the full loyalty oath. He was excused from answering the question: "Are you now, or were you ever, a Communist?"

Now, although senators sometimes complain about the number of generals in Washington, it should not be necessary to take up the time of five of them whenever the future of a former Communist is at stake. There could be simpler methods. Yet it is significant that it was understanding by the generals as to what impelled Leo Kaye to get in and get out of the party that influenced their decision. The theory that once a Communist always a suspect just did not hold when they looked at the real facts.

The understanding of home influences as well as the experiences and emotional development of children must be combined. For many years the Communist party in the United States had made special efforts to enlist youth. This has led to the exaggeration: "Better one member of the Young Communist League than ten members of the party."

Membership for youth is undoubtedly a profound emotional experience. Whether the leaders are aware of it or not, theirs is a determined effort to break down the parental and religious ties of the new member. Only then can Stalin be set up in place of Father and Russia in place of Mother. Perhaps this explains why Communist writers, long after the fashion has died out among others, still like to write the stereotyped fiction in which Father is always a louse or a souse and Mother either a bitch or a fool.

Of course the party attracts children who feel that there is something to this. In very few cases which came to our attention did the children dare tell their parents of the party membership. Except, of course, where the parents were Communists, too. But when the child did tell, there are signs in the way they describe the fact, or in the words themselves, that indicate that they were glad of the hurt inflicted upon the elders.

When the parents did learn about the child's communism, the general reaction was one of shame and fear. The horrid fact was concealed if possible, much as an earlier generation sought to conceal evidence of insanity in a child. Seldom did the parents consult any outsider, teacher, doctor, or clergyman, but handled the situation in such clumsy fashion that the child was driven further into the party for support and companionship. There are some cases where parents seem to have handled the situation wisely enough to permit the child to retrace the steps leading to the party. Scorn, contempt, and anger were missing from the attitude shown by these parents, whatever they may have felt. Often these are parents who in their youth did battle against the domination of equally strong parents.

It is these parents that society might well copy, not only for the benefit of the children but of society itself.

~~~~~~~~~~~~~~~~~~~~~~~~~~~~~~~

CHAPTER SIX

IDEALISTS WITHOUT ILLUSIONS

THE technique of the Big Lie has been so exhaustively explained ever since the Nazis made it part of their admitted strategy that almost everyone with whom anyone disagrees has been accused of using it. Despite repeated exposures, it remains repeatedly successful. Communists, even while arguing that their own aggressions and injustices were necessary, have been able to win a certain amount of belief for their loudly and repeatedly voiced claims to stand for peace and social justice. Some of the believers have found out only later that this means a very special kind of peace and a very odd kind of social justice.

It is at this point that the Communist is redeemable. Our mistake as a nation has been to fail to capitalize on his disillusionment. For in most Communists—in virtually all of the general membership, we believe—there is a strong strain of idealism. Whatever other factors may be involved in their adherence to the party, they are selfless, dedicated people. Furthermore, they have illusions when they join. An idealist with illusions may be almost anything from saint to sinner. It is when he is without illusions but retains his ideals that he becomes the most useful citizen. In reclaiming Communists, the trick is to remove the illusions without impairing the ideals.

Some Communists have done this for themselves when or after they left the party. Some lost both. Then they are left with little purpose and no direction.

Sidney W—, thanks to his ideals and the loss of his illusions, has built a busy, valuable, and (we think) really happy life on the ruins of his old Communist affiliation. Able, intelligent, and persuasive, he was an extremely desirable member from the party's point of view, and even more desirable for a free society. Here is his story:

"I joined the Communist party in the early thirties. I was 24 at the time and worked for the federal government. Probably the thing that pushed me into the party was that I felt terribly guilty at being employed when there were so many unemployed.

"There was also the fact that as the son of a trade-union leader, I had grown up with a great awareness of the plight of the underdog. My father was a worker in the building industry, which gave him highly seasonal employment. We never starved but we never managed to do more than get along by the skin of our teeth. There was always an atmosphere of economic tension in our home.

"My father was a Socialist and sent us all to the Young People's Socialist League Sunday school. When I was 15 I left school and went to work. At the same time I became a member of the Young People's Socialist League in my own right. I had done a lot of reading and a lot of thinking and this was an important conscious deliberate choice on my part. My brothers and my sister have never been politically active. I guess my older brother discovered sex before I did, and Saturday-night dates made getting to the Y.P.S.L. Sunday school too tough for him. As for my sister, I think she's generally aware of a vague difference between the Democratic and Republican parties, but that's about the limit of her political knowledge. My younger brother just never has been particularly excited about politics. My mother was a housewife who never knew or cared much about politics until after I had become a Communist and talked her into marching in parades and demonstrations. She didn't like the idea of war and since I had told her that the Communists were against it, too, she became an enthusiastic demonstrator.

"As far as my relationship with my father was concerned, I loved him very much when I didn't see him and hated him passionately when I was in his presence. I think this was probably true of my brothers and sister, too, but I was more like my father than the others and both my admiration for him and my resistance to him were greater."

So far this is the typical story of the relatively small number of Communists who were children of radical or liberal workers in the American Labor Movement. Sidney's idealistic reaction to his father's beliefs was not unusual either. He continues:

"I got fed up with the Socialist party after listening to them talk incessantly for 10 years and do nothing. I owed much of my knowledge of communism to the Socialists because they spent a lot of time attacking the Communists which I felt might have been better spent in a concrete program of action. A lot of Socialists switched over to the Communist party during the depression because, like me, they believed the Communists were the only group prepared to do something about the terrible economic conditions beside just talk. Moreover, the Socialists lacked the advantage of having a Soviet Union to point to as a shining example of what could be achieved by the defeat of capitalism. I might add at this point that I had always been an extremely nationalistic guy—probably another inheritance from my immigrant father, who had a great loyalty to his adopted land.

"My difficulties with the party began when I went to Spain to fight with the Lincoln Brigade. The trouble probably started with the fact that I have a gift for languages. I learned to speak Spanish and to read it fluently in a fairly short time. As a result, I was able to read the Spanish papers and to talk to Spaniards.

"I began correcting my previous conception of the Spanish situation which I had gotten completely from the American Communist party. I learned, for example, that the Popular Front was a hoax. Nobody believed in it except schmoes who had never learned to read Spanish. I found that while the other groups in the Popular Front were adhering to its terms, the Communists were going right ahead and doing the very things they had agreed not to do which made the Popular Front possible. For example, none of the member organizations were supposed to recruit, proselytize, or use high-pressure tactics to win new members. The Communists were the only group which consistently violated this agreement. They viewed the Popular Front solely as an instrumentality, and used it accordingly. They gave lip-service to the Popular Front idea and did just enough grandstand stuff to enable them to point with pride to their militant devotion to the Popular Front. The difference between what the party professed to do and what it really did made it pretty confusing for me for a while until the whole thing began to emerge in my own mind for what it was—probably one of the worst examples of organized large-scale hypocrisy in history.

"During this period when I was trying to sort things out in my own mind, I started getting in trouble at party meetings of the Brigade. I sounded off on a number of issues and rapidly became unpopular. Luckily I had a couple of old friends who had risen to important posts in the party who came to my defense when my deviationist attitude was reported, with reassurances that I was just a slightly crazy guy, not a disrupter or a spy. Dozens of boys in the Lincoln Brigade were executed for deviationist tendencies, sometimes on the pretext that they were deserters.

"When I got back to the United States in 1938, I was intellectually certain of where I stood with regard to the party. I didn't sever my connection, however, immediately in the sense of formally resigning. I just stopped going to meetings. The Friends of the Lincoln Brigade at that time had a tremendous amount of money at their disposal which was supposed to be used to help veterans. I made two speeches for them for which I was paid, but after that they obviously didn't trust me not to shoot my mouth off and didn't give me any more speaking engagements.

"After a few months I was notified to appear before the Control Commission. This was the disciplinary body which investigated grievances against members, carried on personnel investigations, and selected people for special duty or Comintern work. Notices to appear before the Commission were never sent out by mail, but by word of mouth. When the message reached you, you either kept the appointment or left town or just holed up and worried yourself to death, depending on what kind of a guy you were. I kept the appointment. I had no intention of making a big dramatic thing out of it and going into details of why I could no longer accept the party line. I just played indifferent. The man who interviewed me was very solicitous at first.

" 'What's the matter, comrade? Aren't you feeling well?'

"He said I was probably suffering from shell shock and

offered to arrange for me to have a long vacation at Camp Kinderland, the party country resort. He held out the lure of possible re-employment by the party; I didn't have a job at the time. When none of this broke down the indifferent attitude I had assumed, he warned me that if I didn't pull myself together and start behaving properly, I would be expelled. Nobody had to explain to me what this involved. For people like me it meant complete ostracism and being cut off from all of the people who had been my friends. Even though I was sure where I stood in principle, I must admit this prospect gave me many hours of doubt as to what I should do. At some points I was almost convinced that the fault was with me, that it was my weakness not any defect in the party that was precipitating the break.

"The ostracism was as bad as my worst anticipations. Men I had lived with passed me on the street without speaking to me. Even a man whose life I had saved in Spain refused to talk to me. He had been wounded in battle, and I carried him to safety on my back for 15 kilometers from early morning to sunset, holding my pants up with one hand because I had used my belt as a tourniquet for his arm. The first time I met him on the street after my interview with the Commission, he passed me by. The second time, he couldn't stand it and asked me to have a cup of coffee with him. He justified himself by saying:

" 'I stick to the party.'

"Once that was off his chest, he never talked to me again. Things were so bad that I became suspicious of the few people who would still talk to me. I thought they had probably been assigned to keep tabs on me.

"Up to this point I had continued attending meetings of the Veterans of the Lincoln Brigade. While I still had no wish for an open clash with the party, I had not been able to sit quietly and watch the men who had fought fascism in Spain follow the pro-Fascist party line of neutrality toward the war in Europe. This was, of course, well before the invasion of Russia caused an overnight switch in the line.

"I suddenly found myself brought up on charges for expulsion from the Veterans of the Lincoln Brigade. To my astonishment I found my importance blown up to fantastic proportions. Earl Browder was the chief speaker against me. He called me the successor to Trotsky and described me as a cunning manipulator who had cultivated a bland exterior to cover up his devious and widespread machinations. The charges were seconded by John Gates, who delivered a speech reporting practically every word I had ever said during the years in Spain. He even had a detailed account of a meeting at which I had queried La Passionaria's evaluation of a certain battle. [She was the fiery woman leader of Spanish Communists.] It was one of those damned petty semantic squabbles that people sometimes get into. But to hear Gates tell it, I was a disrupter whose object had been to lose the war in Spain. When I tried to speak in self-defense, I was physically escorted to the door.

"I felt very strongly on the subject of the war in Europe. I saw it as a direct continuation of what we had been fighting in Spain. After Dunkirk when it looked as though the Nazis were going to overrun Europe, I wanted to go up to Canada and enlist, but couldn't for personal reasons. I got a job instead, regained a little humility, and, incidentally, got married. I enlisted in the army immediately after the attack on Pearl Harbor.

"After the war I got a job working for a union. They didn't ask about my background. The person who recommended me for the job said that I was all right politically and the union took it at that. Later on, the full story of my background became known to the people with whom I work, but I have never found that it was held against me.

"It seems to me that the fear of leaving the party is largely engendered by the party itself and the threats that were made to people who left. The reign of terror started long before the popular Communist hunt. The Communists strongly established the myth that there was no middle road. 'If you're not with us, you're against us.' There were only two kinds of people—Communists and rabid reactionaries. A lot of us believed that. And there were just enough ex-Communists who had become Hearst writers to make it seem as if this was really the choice. The spectacle of the men who had really gone reactionary was unappealing enough to make a man want to avoid doing the same. The only decent self-respecting alternative that seemed to be open to an ex-Communist was to lie low and do absolutely nothing.

"I got a very vivid picture of this around the time of Dunkirk when a few other veterans of the Lincoln Brigade and I tried in vain to salvage a little of the integrity of the organization by organizing an opposition group to fight what we considered its pro-Fascist stand. The men we tried to organize were not neutral on the issue; on the contrary, they were bitter about it, but they wouldn't express it in action. They only wanted to be let alone. Maybe they still had a feeling of guilt about leaving the party. While I am certainly not condoning the witch hunt of the last few years, I think it is the attitudes which the party builds up rather than what outsiders do that makes it difficult for members to quit."

Of course the party tries to keep people from getting out. All the more reason why we should make it easier. It may be added that among the contributors to our collection of stories by former Communists, Sidney, a man of ability, judgment, and high ideals, is in a very small minority in believing that the party's threats are more effective than society's attitudes in preventing withdrawal.

By way of contrast to his story, it might be worth looking at the account of one who may be said to have lost his ideals but retained his illusions. Richard Q— had rather high ideals to start with, too.

Brought up in a small Midwestern town where his parents were the wealthiest or almost the wealthiest residents, he had an income of his own sufficient to support him comfortably. He has never married, but spent many years in college—long enough to take two time-consuming graduate degrees which have fitted him for his chosen career of teaching and economics. His parents were indifferent to politics, and apparently to social problems, too.

Richard was nearly 30, approaching the second of his two graduate degrees, when he joined the Communist party. He had not been in college all that time—there had been an interval of teaching. Although his early manhood had been spent in the depression, he did not join the party until that phenomenon was well past for most people, although he thinks his reason for becoming a Communist was a desire "to belong to a group that was following a plan to lessen unemployment." He explains:

"When I joined in 1938, all the U.S. had been facing unemployment for many years, and for many of us a desire to find a solution had become very strong. The CP offered a policy of a united front with all groups who wanted to work together to move toward ending monopolies and increasing public works. The Socialists I knew would not speak to the Communists and I thought I was joining the group with the less narrow approach to economic problems. Also I was persuaded by reading that sudden change would be less upsetting to all concerned than gradual change, so I wanted to help more and more people to see the value of a change in the economic organization, which the majority would then adopt.

"For a year before joining I felt I was a coward not to take a more definite stand of some sort. The phrase 'you are responsible for what you do not do as well as for what you do' kept going through my mind.

"The day I decided I must act was a day that a conservative professor had given a particularly futile analysis of how to control monopolies and their effects on prices and jobs. That was in the spring of 1938, but I did not seek out local leaders until the fall of 1938.

"What I saw of the party was not controlled by an outside country; what the papers say now was what the party in 1938 taught is not what the party as I knew it taught in 1938. I was somewhat repelled by the secrecy at the time, but one member of my family and one friend outside the party knew at the time that I belonged. During my two years as a dues-paying member I participated in discussions and in some distribution of literature, but was completely inactive for a year before definitely not supporting the party.

"Membership gave me a group with which to discuss the things I cared about, openly and fully. I did not take many opinions from the party; guess I was not a good member. While in the party, I did not feel great limitation of freedom of discussion, but I was in a college-graduate group.

"After two years, factors not present when I joined the party were acting to lessen unemployment. Beside the change in the employment level, I was also not too sympathetic with the party stand *re* Willkie and international support for the British.

"My final decision, in the fall of 1941, not to renew contact with the party was motivated directly by a desire to work under civil service and a fear of not being able to argue that the party was not subversive. In addition, in the fall of 1941 the government adopted a new oath *re* membership in subversive organizations. A move to a new city made it possible to leave without definite action.

"Since my experience is not known, it has not openly affected my getting a job, but I now feel I cannot answer civil service form 57 [application for employment] and get a job. Since I think most people trust me, I feel I might be a liability to those I work with if my experience is made known.

"Since I left, I have felt more strongly the importance of freedom of speech and seen more clearly that the party does not urge such freedom in Russia. Were I to choose, I would have remained out primarily because of the lack of an allegiance to freedom of speech by the party. I never accepted the theory of labor value nor certain other Marxist principles."

If Richard seems to be rather more timid and less devoted to principle than most of those who explain their reasons for joining and leaving the Communist party, it may be that he is more honest in appraising himself, or more humble.

Robert O— is much more the revolutionary type who, in the minds of most people, is the real Communist. Born and raised on a farm, he was the only child of his father's second marriage, which had taken place when old Mr. O— was past 50. Robert had five older half brothers and sisters by his father's first wife.

"As a child," Robert recalls, "I enjoyed all of the necessities of life, including plenty of books and newspapers, but few luxuries. My father's income bracket—impossible to describe in terms of dollars—was typical of farm owners who do their own work and never employ labor."

Mr. O— also added slightly to his income by teaching school and serving as minister of the local church, but it was the contribution to the education and religion of the rural community of which he was a part rather than the pay that seems to have interested him. One of his older sons was a teacher and editor. In that atmosphere, Robert had rather precocious literary tastes which led him to revolutionary ideas.

"I joined the Young People's Socialist League about the age of 13 or 14, as a member at large," he writes. "I had been a student of the writings of Marx, Engels, Bebel, Kautsky, etc., since approximately age 12. The influence of the Russian Revolution of 1917 [he was then 14] was strong. I believed that the first Socialist country would pave the way for the rest of mankind. My information on that revolution from 1917 to 1920 was obtained primarily from books by John Reed, M. J. Olgin, Albert Rhys Williams, and the left-Socialist and Communist press. Reading stories about Spartacus, *Uncle Tom's Cabin*, Robert Blatchford's *Not Guilty*, histories of the French Revolution by Thiers and others, between the ages of 7 and 12, led me to a feeling of revolt against all forms of class rule and oppression. From earliest childhood I resented discrimination against Negroes and all minorities. Influenced by reading Thoreau, especially his 'Essay on the Duty of Civil Disobedience.' Reading popular Socialist literature like the *Appeal to Reason, Melting Pot, Ripsaw, Milwaukee Leader, Intercollegiate Socialist Review,* and the *Communist Manifesto, Value, Price and Profit, Wage, Labor and Capital,* plus some popular booklets by Algernon Lee, Morris Hillquit, and others prepared me for more advanced study of Marxian economic and philosophical theories."

It is small wonder that Robert was graduated young from high school and that in his first job he was strongly influenced by his early reading. He worked as a factory hand, as a clerk, and finally on newspapers, becoming editorial writer for a small city daily when he was 20. He was soon fired because of the radical tone of his editorials although the word radical may here as in many cases be no more than a synonym for "controversial."

Moving across the country in search of new fields, he was horrified by a first-hand view of a particularly brutal example of strike breaking in the early 1920's. Robert threw himself into the cause of the workers with such enthusiasm that he was sentenced to a 40-year jail term. This was reduced to three years and "made me ready to become a disciplined member of the Communist party." He applied for membership on his release and was welcomed, for he had become something of a hero as a result of his trial and imprisonment. For the next 15 years he was devoted to party work, "to the full extent of my time and physical strength." Most of the time he was a paid party worker, assigned to editing, writing, and organizing jobs of sufficient importance to make him one of the secondary group of national leaders, far closer to the inner circle than the rank-and-file members who are the bulk of our cases. His peak salary, incidentally, was $37.50 a week.

"At the time of my party membership," he explained, "I certainly thought the movement offered the *only hope* for society. I had little thought of any personal benefit; like most party leaders, I thought the chances of living through the world war and revolutions necessary to bring about the world union of Soviet Socialist Republics and

to raise the Red Flag in America, the last fortress of capitalism, would be very slight. We were ready to give our lives 'for the movement' and the 'emancipation of mankind.' "

In this state of idealistic illusions, probably no one but another Communist could have interested Robert matrimonially. At any rate, about three years after he joined the party he married another party member. Together they worked for the cause in many parts of the country, but she usually had to take a factory job to make ends meet, as she was not paid. Even after their children were born, they continued the same mobile life. Wherever they went, most of their friends were party members.

Nevertheless, Robert says he was having "secret differences with party leadership" as early as 1933. Then came "the liquidation of Bukharin, Tukhachevsky, and other leaders I had personally known." Just before his marriage, Robert had made a visit to the Soviet Union, and saw rather more of it than most visitors in the several months of his stay. He was not inclined to doubt the value of the Soviet system from anything he saw, however, but seems to have been impressed enormously by the meetings he attended and the people he met. He felt himself in at the beginning of a great new era in history. When some of the men who were to make that world were purged, he hesitated. Or at least so he thinks now. Actually he did not get out of the party for nearly eight years. He managed to go along with the rapid shifts of the party line through the anti-Fascist stage, through the period of the Stalin-Hitler pact, through the beginnings of the war alliance with the democracies after Hitler attacked Russia. But Robert was losing his illusions rapidly.

"There was increasing disillusionment and dissatisfaction during the last three years in the party," he says.

Even without illusions it was hard to leave. Mrs. O— was disillusioned, too, which made it easier, but they would be leaving their friends, their work, and embarking upon a difficult quest for jobs and security. They were not ready to see in communism an enemy to be fought.

"I left the party," says Robert, "by ceasing to attend meetings and pay dues, and by giving evasive answers to Steve Nelson and other top leaders who tried to force me to return to membership and activity.

"In leaving the Communist party I knew that I was facing a real physical danger—of murder by the agents of the GPU, or NKVD, of sharing the fate of Juliet Stuart Poyntz, once a personal friend, Trotsky, Krivitsky, Munzenberg, and so many others. Also, I expected and correctly that the party would use its great power to force me from jobs. And I knew that most professed 'anti-Communists' would not really and sincerely accept the support of those most able to help—the former members of the party.

"After leaving the party, an adjustment period of about six years was necessary to overcome remnants of 'Communist' ideology. Technically speaking, 'communism' should be used in quotation marks, for under the Stalin dictatorship there is neither communism nor any 'advance' in that direction. And it can be called socialism only by such distortions of words as the use of the term 'people's democracies.' "

Robert thinks that the long delay between the time of his growing disillusionment and his withdrawal from the party was largely due to the rather dismal fate of most ex-Communists of whom he knew anything. They were frequently reviled in the press and of course were vilified by their former comrades. Robert adds:

"My decision to come out *publicly* in 1949 had been delayed for years by that factor. In fact, if—in the light of my own experiences—I had it all to do over again, I probably would not have the courage to defy Stalin and his powerful apparatus in this country and throughout the world. Even as a party member, I lived better than since I have testified openly against the party. There has been no economic security for me; and I know this is true of most ex-party members, especially former leaders."

From his experience with Communist groups in many parts of the country and his own experience in getting new members—"I recruited hundreds," he says—Robert has noted that in the Southern communities, especially where there were groups of Negroes recruited, a substantial number of Communist members were underprivileged workers and farmers. In some cases, he says, these were more than half. On the other hand, in the far West, he worked in a county with about 400 members. About half of them were labor union officials or members, the members fairly evenly divided between CIO and AF of L unions. About 75 party members were professional men and women. The rest were housewives and university students.

"From the largest national minority group in the county, Portuguese, we had three members of a total of 20,000 in the county. With a Spanish-Mexican population of 15,000 there were some thousands of 'oakies'—immigrants from Oklahoma. *Not one* of them belonged to the CP! Of the county membership one might say that about half were of average income and half above average, with an insignificant number below."

Robert contrasts this with a Southern county at about the same time where the party had 1,200 members. He says

"At least 800 were Negro, mostly sharecroppers. Many of the white members were textile workers. Intellectuals professionals, and highly skilled workers did not number more than 200 of the 1,200 members. But they furnished more than half of the District Committee members."

These figures on Negro membership, it must be said, are far higher than other authorities in or out of the party give. If there were 800 Negro members in one county, that would have been nearly half the total membership in the country for their race.

On methods used to recruit party members, Robert says: "I had no special formula and the approach varied according to economic conditions, background, education, organizational affiliations, etc., of each person. For intellectuals the approach usually was based on dialectical materialism and other theoretical foundations—the more abstract the better. Trade unionists usually were brought into the party by promoting physical clashes with police forces. Nothing makes a Communist of a worker as quickly as a policeman's club. Selfish and narrow-minded industrialists are the best assistants for Stalin in his plans for world conquest. In general, the capitalists of America are far less alert to the dangers of communism than the industrial workers. Few people know how to fight communism effectively. The ex-Communists know how, but with the present attitude of government, press, and public only a few of the very brave or the very foolish will risk their economic security and their lives to do so."

Robert thinks it is impossible to generalize as to why people join and leave the party. He points out that there is no magic formula either way, but:

"If I had to make a generalization, I would say: people join the Communist party for hundreds of individual reasons and combinations of them, primarily because of the *religious* appeal of the world's *first atheistic religion,* and its utopian promise of a society on earth free from all of the human weaknesses we all know only too well. Some remain in the party, becoming fanatics and shells of their former selves—as blind to realities as any religious martyr in history. Others become disillusioned, realizing that Soviet communism is a combination of state capitalism and slavery and is an imminent threat to everything of value in civilization."

The idealist in Robert notes how strong is what he calls the "religious appeal" of communism. Members of what the world recognizes as more orthodox churches than communism will hardly like the use of the word "religious" in this connection. But it is not at all farfetched. The idealists recognize it; what of the men and women who thought Marx was God and Lenin and Stalin were his prophets—and then found that this was a false religion after all? They, too, are a chapter in the search for what makes Communists, and unmakes them.

~~~~~~~~~~~~~~~~~~~~~~~~~~~~~~~~~~

CHAPTER SEVEN

BIGOTS AND BELIEVERS

Every religion attracts two kinds of people—bigots and believers. They seem to be beneficent or evil in the world in proportion to the predominance of one or the other. Yet it is sometimes difficult to tell which is which. Eric Hoffer, for instance, has written one of the most popular of modern philosophical books in the field and called it *The True Believer*. Yet what he has done is to draw a portrait of the bigot; the believer scarcely enters his pages. Fanaticism and faith are two different things.

Communism, like the Ku Klux Klan, fascism, and nazism, has a great appeal to the bigot. It is more akin to nazism than to the Klan, and in Europe the members of both parties have found it easy to switch their allegiance from one to another. Communism supplied some of Hitler's best storm troopers. Nazism supplied some of Russia's most useful tools in the Iron Curtain countries. The characteristics of these people are well put by Hoffer when he says:

"All mass movements generate in their adherents a readiness to die and a proclivity for united action; all of them, irrespective of the doctrine they preach and the program they project, breed fanaticism, enthusiasm, fervent hope, hatred and intolerance; all of them are capable of releasing a powerful flow of activity in certain departments of life; all of them demand blind faith and singlehearted allegiance."

It is this fanaticism which seems to enable the Communist in America to accept blindly the bewildering shifts in Soviet policy, to shout hosannah today and crucify tomorrow, while retaining the conviction that both positions are taken for the positive good of mankind. It is this fanaticism which finally brings some Communists to the point of betraying their country, firm in the conviction that they are doing it to save the world. Obviously there is a wide gap between walking in a picket line or handing out leaflets or planning a worker's state or even engaging in violence during a strike and actually spying on behalf of a foreign government. The step that bridges that gap is one which seems to be taken easily enough once the point is reached. But the actual spying often seems very much out of character.

This is a new kind of spy in American history. In the past, we have had our own spies in purely military ways— and some of them are national heroes. Our enemies had the same kind. Each side also had spies who were motivated entirely by money, and some who preferred the enemy and became deserters. But here is a spy whose fanaticism leads him to set himself entirely apart from national loyalties on either side. By some psychological gymnastics, he convinces himself that the welfare of mankind is linked to the success of another country.

Obviously not all members of the party enter this stage, and not all know much about it. So far as we can judge, however, the beginnings of the future spy in the party are not much different from that of the other members. Perhaps almost anyone with the necessary amount of bigotry in his make-up could go as far.

This fanaticism or bigotry also seems to make tolerable for many Communists the system of suspicion and internal spying that is a feature of any such underground movement. Not all party members are capable of doing this; some dislike the whole idea of secrecy, but even when they recognize it as what many have told us is an obviously necessary evil, they do not carry it to the point of spying on their fellow members. These seem to be the ones who, after they leave, are most reluctant to give testimony as to who was in the party when they were. After all, "squealing" and "tale-bearing" are among the major sins which children can commit against each other. In all American groups the young learn to despise both, and it is not easy for anyone except a fanatic to overcome such early training.

Of course, the whole matter of secrecy and mystery has its attractions as well as its repulsions. Again, every child has enjoyed having secrets with his fellows, and against all the rest of the world. Many a Communist, according to the experience of those former members who have talked to us, has been intrigued by this and also by the fact that he never knew the identity of many Communists. The cell system of organization prevents the rank-and-file member from knowing party members outside his own group. He does not even know definitely who the Russian overlords of the party in this country might be. And he enjoys this secrecy to the extent that he has the qualifications of bigotry within him. In this he is much like the Klansman, who hides his identity under a sheet. The chief difference in this respect is that the Klansman at least supports the cotton industry by using a goodly amount of cloth to preserve his secret.

The bigotry of the Klan and kindred organizations is much like that of the Communist in many respects. However, in general the man under the hood is badly and little educated, relatively poor, and without much prospect for material advancement—just the opposite of most Communists. But both groups are composed of individuals with a belief in absolutes, and a real need to have issues solved for them in absolute terms. They both believe that all who disagree with them are wicked, not just mistaken. They need a scapegoat. The one fixes on the Jew or the Negro or the Catholic. The other pins all ills on the capitalist and the capitalist's evil minions.

Both, too, are individuals who have been unable to solve their personal problems. In order to escape from a sense of frustration in this regard, they turn to a movement which puts them in touch with great power. They need that feeling of being identified with the force which will rule the world or at least the city or state.

One big difference between the reactionary bigot and the radical bigot should be noted. The reactionary is afraid of real change; he wants above all to keep what he has got, and only when he thinks that is secure will he reach out timidly for the world. He stands on his little bit of earth, clutching his possessions, and is afraid to move. The radical dislikes, even hates, what is and welcomes change because he is not afraid for himself. He is more flexible, in a sense adventurous. Thus the reactionary does not want to move from his community, even if it is poor, nor change his job nor follow unfamiliar leaders. The radical bigot, because he dislikes what he has, is willing and even happy to leave it for a new town and a new job. When the Communist party orders a young member with a sick wife, a new baby, and no savings to throw up his job and move halfway across the country, he packs his few belongings and sets out gladly.

Paul J— as a Communist welcomed privations cheerfully, but now that he is out of the party he likes his comforts and wants to keep them. Well educated and from a cultured home whose members were what he calls "stout liberals," he was attending a private school when his father died. Mr. J— left enough money to provide well for his son's continued education. Paul thinks he joined the party "out of intellectual excitement in order to make a better world." He says:

"I became very active, and in fact made a living as a party official. It was not much of a living but I did not mind the deprivation because I felt very important. You must remember that the people in the party are selfless financially and really think they are going to make the world over. I took personal risks of jail and persecution which I know I never would have taken in order to make a fortune. I also wanted to prove to my father that it was not enough to be a liberal.

"While a member of the party I studied party literature and in fact no other literature. I was taught to be critical of any other writing or speech, a habit which was aggravated by the constant degradation of Communist members who in their writings did not adhere to the party line. My jobs in the party were increasingly more important and I met my then heroes.

"The party shifted me around from one city to another to do various jobs, and I gladly accepted these orders. But I also remember the fight I had with my father as to which college I should go to out of town."

Paul was married but that did not bother him in his moves, for his wife also was a member of the party. But after several years, the blind fanaticism of his earlier days in the party faded. He was no longer willing to accept un-questioningly the reading of nothing except Communist literature.

"At the time I started to think of getting out," he says, "I rationalized my reasons in the sense of thinking in terms of free speech, Czechoslovakia, etc. I now know that this was mere rationalization. The Stalin-Hitler pact had not jarred me at all."

Paul does not think he was unusual in accepting the low income of a party member.

"Out of hundreds of members I met, I only recall about half a dozen who could not make at least $5,000 a year," he says. "This does not mean that they were making that much while in the party, nor does it mean that they were unhappy while in the party because of their small income. It is hard work to be a party member. At the lowest levels, they keep you sweating, but the sweat gives you a feeling of being effective."

Even as Paul accepted the party line of his reading, Thomas Y— confined his friendships entirely to the party during his eight years in it, which did not end until near the close of World War II. His family background was much like that of Paul, except that he had more brothers and sisters. He joined the party while he was a graduate student, and remained in it for the first years of his career as a teacher.

Thomas joined the party at a time, he says, when it "was waging a fight against fascism." He remained in it and active—in fact he worked very hard and "though not in the inner circle I was considered a leader"—all through the years of the party line's most tortuous shifts. His family made no difficulties for him; they thought his membership was his business, he reports. But as the war drew toward

its close, he felt that the Communist line was
as that which had captured his faith. He writ

"My reasons for getting out were intellect
left was about the beginning of a great exodus
myself who were disgusted with the grow
tendencies within the party. For a t
of bureaucracy became patent, it
which I believed. I'm glad I'm
I despise the Louis Budenz

"I have felt that, since
has been characterized
tive side of my eight
me good grounding in
I am still in sympath⸱   ⸱ⅽally a
philosophical mater   ⸱⸱ fact unquestionably
contributed to my ⸱⸱⸱⸱⸱⸱ng the party."

As to his life since then, Thomas comments:

"It has been difficult for me to hold a job, for the 'Mc-
Carthy type' of person has pursued me. I have made quite
a new life, with primary reference to friends and social
acquaintances, but not totally new."

Thomas and Paul show evidences of belief quite as much
as of bigotry, and this element of communism should not
be neglected or minimized. In fact, it would seem that the
party has enlisted many who in the age of religious wars
would have been the most intolerant persecutors on one
side or another. The belief leads them to look for something positive; the bigotry prevents them, once they have
found the positive feature, from admitting that there can
be any truth in another's beliefs.

There are points of similarity between the party and
some highly organized religions. Both demand complete
respect for and obedience to a higher power. Both filter
the commands of that power down through official spokes-

ove all, both demand in the follower an un-
aith in dogma which cannot be proved. Min-
een among the most vocal in deploring that
s do not satisfy today many people who want
These people are impatient for results. They re-
eligion which, to them, consists of listening to ser-
s and going through certain formal observances. They
want to *do* something themselves. They want to prove their
faith by works other than charitable. In the organized religions they find no such works, but in communism their
lives are kept busy with them. And they hear the sermons,
too.

They welcome the great amount of study and indoctri-
nation that goes with initiation into the party. This course
of study is stern and absolute, even to the point where
novices have been afraid to ask questions for fear of being
suspected of deviation—the word which Communists have
adopted as a synonym for heresy. Questioning here, as in
religion, may lead to doubt, and doubt is the enemy of
any faith which pretends to be infallible. Communists
must be even more rigidly orthodox than any religionist
The party has set up mortal men—in effect one mortal
man, Stalin—as the infallible source of all truth. The
church, any church, attributes infallibility only to a higher
power than any man. Now man, to maintain the ascend
ancy of a Stalin, must demand for stricter obedience than
religion requires.

In general, the Communist believer is not especiall
stubborn or obstinate. His fervor gives meaning to his life
and he accepts the party doctrine with all its contradic
tions. There is a sense of fulfillment in the manual work
which is required of the intellectual. Carrying banners
stuffing envelopes, transporting packages of pamphlets, i
a release that is almost like the occupational therapy of

rehabilitation hospital. The harder the work and the longer the hours, the more the members like it. No other organization in America has been able to translate fanaticism into sweat to the same degree.

The practice of flagellation, not unknown in religion, is modified to suit the Communist spirit. Actually, the personality of the Communist seems to be one that looks to castigation for salvation. The membership not only likes to punish, but it likes to be punished. They welcome the scorn of non-Communists; they welcome persecution; they like to think of themselves as the victims of capitalist terror. At the same time, they are severe in meting out punishment to the deviator or the deserter.

The believer, as opposed to the bigot, does not change his faith unless he has been reached by another that appeals to him more powerfully or has been subjected to disillusionment by finding that the practices and preachments are at variance with each other.

Charles F— was a Communist believer and in the opinion of the party a martyr, too. They looked upon him as a Judas before they were through. He is older than most of our subjects, and had a background of radicalism long before he became a Communist.

Born in the last years of the nineteenth century in New England, he was the descendant of farmers for many generations. His father had left the farm for a city job, and the family enjoyed a good if modest income. All the members but Charles were stanch New England Republicans.

The boy went to work in a factory when he was 14—not at all unusual for the sons of New England craftsmen and farmers before World War I. He promptly became involved in the struggle for shorter hours and better conditions, not to mention more pay. By the time he was out of his teens he was a member of the Industrial Workers of the World. He was, therefore, a convert to the idea of revolution and "one big union" long before the Russian Revolution.

As a matter of fact, he joined the Socialist party before he became a Communist, and it was not until the middle 1920's that he was convinced through such speakers as Gitlow, one of the best-known Communist leaders of the time, that Russia was the ideal workers' state. He specifically mentions Gitlow, who went to jail for his Communist beliefs in the 1920's only to become an active fighter against the party later. Charles was still a radical trade unionist, and it seemed to him that neither the Socialist party nor the American Federation of Labor was doing much for the great mass of workers, and very little for the skilled workers.

"During my leadership of one strike in the late 1920's," he says, "I felt the necessity of joining the CP to be able to attend their 'fraction' meetings, which I knew existed. There was more democracy in the CP at that time. So to get down to brass tacks, as the Yankees say, what induced me to join the CP at that time was the propaganda that Russia was a workers' state run for and by the workers and that the CP was a means to organize the bad-off workers in this country. The AF of L was not doing it.

"There have been no Socialists or leftists in my family. The nearest approach: my two brothers now vote the Democratic ticket. I come from a Yankee family. All Republicans. My folks, especially my grandfathers and my *father*, always believed in *free speech*. All my relatives, with the exception of my immediate family, were against me while I was in the Socialist and Communist parties. What kept the pot boiling was the murder of Sacco and Vanzetti. Though my father did not understand what it was all about, he thought they got a raw deal and was with me in this. Also later when I was arrested on a murder charge while organizing a strike. But there was nothing leftist about it. He was against capital punishment.

"International events such as the revolution in Russia, troubled areas in Germany, Italy, etc., all did something to frame my mind for joining the CP. But so did national events. There can be no dispute about it, some very bad conditions existed in this country at that time. Southern workers and minority questions—Communist phrase, eh?—and who was doing anything about it?

"As you know, I met my Waterloo in a particularly vicious strike. I went there to organize the 'slaves'—yes, that is what they were, slaves to the mill owners, and some of them not far from it either. The owners didn't like it a bit. They had been buying off the old-time 'union' organizers. They had no luck with me, so they decided to shoot me out. Well, you know all about the frame-up business then."

What had happened was the killing of a policeman during the strike, and in a bitter and thoroughly prejudiced trial Charles was found guilty and sentenced to a long jail term. He still insists, and most students of the evidence believe, that the other side killed the policeman in order to "get" Charles and break the strike. To continue his own story:

"The CP of course was delighted. The other fellows and myself were in the middle.

"I went to Russia while out on bail. Contrary to some people's contention, I did *not* skip bail. It was my intention to go there while out on bail to see how a workers' state was functioning. I found out it was *not* a workers' state, the workers were *not* running the works, and there was *no* freedom as we understand freedom. Things were in a hell of a mess. I then and there decided to leave the party—according to the Communists one does not leave, one is expelled. Furthermore, I felt I should tell the workers in the United States about what I saw. I was about the first that had been a member of the party; Gitlow, Budenz, and many others who later 'confessed' were still there or near it. I did not hesitate getting out and doing this although I knew it meant the loss of friends in America; the only ones I had were in the party. But, as I said, I thought I owed it to the workers in the United States to tell the truth no matter what it did to me. So I came back.

"The CP certainly did their damnedest against me, with the help too of their fellow travelers and wishy-washy liberals who chimed in with the Communists against me. I know it is easier *today* to get out. Quite popular, in fact.

"I place it as the early 1930's when I finally made the official break to get out of the party with a public statement, so I was in the party five years. It should be mentioned here that an honest person could not possibly get away from the party like one turning off a faucet. I went to the Trotsky groups but never joined any of the various sects. In fact I thought they were just frustrated Stalinits . . . that was misspelled by error, but I can see it is a good word coined accidentally—Stalinitwits. And it seems to me—and I love Norman Thomas—that the Socialists are just *frustrated*.

"After the Stalinists turned me in to the police—they were powerful those days—I served four years for a crime I did not commit. When I got out the Communists were still powerful, in fact more so. They held important jobs in unions and the government, the Lord High Executioners. They tried to keep me from getting work, and if it was not for the I.L.G.W. Union (Dubinsky) I certainly would have been hard put to it for work. I worked then for six years, until the plant closed down.

"These things work havoc with me and I have not been the same since. I traveled around the country speaking against the Communists, started out when they were in their heyday because I did not want them to get control of the unions. The curious angle now is that I still am out of work and no union will take me on as an organizer *because* I was a Communist.

"The moral of this story would seem to be: it is safer to stay—silent—in the CP."

Of course Charles himself has lived another moral: that a man's beliefs are more important to him than safety. To us his story suggests still another: that the Communist believer, as opposed to the Communist bigot, can be brought out of the party into genuine social usefulness if society will take the trouble to make plain to him that other causes are more deserving of his devotion.

Without that effort by society, too many former Communists will avoid participation in the progress to which they might contribute. Leonard W—, for example, represents a fairly large group of those who, joining the party for a variety of the emotional reasons already discussed, are chiefly motivated in leaving it by loss of their belief. Well-to-do, chafing against his own inability to stand up to a forceful father, he became a Communist while he was in college, "sort of slid in," as he puts it. For a time his faith was well nurtured. He says:

"All of us submitted ourselves and our lives as if we were entering a holy order. We were not seduced into the party; we begged to join.

"In the party we asked no questions. Our main active emotion was envy of the leaders in our own cells or at big party rallies. We read, we studied, we worked. We worked for an end, the only kind of work worth while. Everyone screened and appraised everyone else. We spied on each other—not in a personal way, we thought, but for the sake of that new sunrise for all men and women. This goal was so great that we understood that there had to be discipline; there could be no opposition. No crusade can afford deviations, opposition, or even questioning. The ultimate revolution must depend, we believed, on unquestioned submission to the word from Stalin. We were dedicated, and don't minimize the joy of dedication.

"Yesterday was irrelevant, today insignificant, only tomorrow counted. As with all fanatic, blind efforts, if you once join in the band, each one helps carry the other along.

"All my loyalties became wrapped into the party; my home, my school, my college, my fraternity, my father, my mother didn't count. They were either people to be used or enemies to be ultimately destroyed. Above all, I surrendered my belief in the gospel of the open mind.

"It would be a mistake to underestimate the satisfaction of party work and of party sacrifice. Those who give more than their food bills permit to a church or an orphanage or a hospital well know what I write about. There is a kind of deep feeling of well-being that comes from making something sacred, which I guess is the real root of sacrifice. The sacrifices usually open to the well-to-do are limited. Their gifts of money or time are meaningless in the sense of giving something one deeply desires to retain. My generous father and mother died without experiencing sacrifice in this sense. To give up another Cadillac for a letter of thanks from a hospital or church may be sweet, but requires a different word to describe it than sacrifice.

"For my part, I understood the general run of members. I was fortunate enough emotionally and economically to afford the luxury of trying to persuade those I worked with to get out when I got out. I told them it was an infantile movement, particularly for upper-middle-class, upper-educated Americans. We were being used as expendable dupes. Our motives were of the best, that is, no thought of financial gain or outward social rewards. We must have been sick as the kleptomaniac is ill, that is, the kleptomaniac who does not resell the stolen goods. Thus do I distinguish the professionals from the innocent lambs."

The notion of illness occurs to many former Communists, but they suffer from a disease only in the metaphorical sense. In Leonard's case, he got out of the party after what he calls "a period of nagging doubt." He has attempted no other crusade. He told his story to the authorities through his attorney, but he wanted no personal appearances.

"Moreover, to what end should I make a grandstand disclosure?" he asked. "It was unnecessary to vindicate my own conversion. No. I rather doubt the full conversion of those who talk too much and too often and too publicly and for too much money."

By far the most attractive qualities of the Communist and the former Communist are their idealism and their faith. There may be a certain amount of hypocrisy and self-deception in them, as there is in many other people, but for the most part, we are convinced, the sentiments are sincere, genuine.

The party knows very well the human material it can draw into the rank and file. The leaders capitalize on the ideals and the search for a satisfying belief which characterizes so many of their recruits, especially the young. But not all idealists and believers are good prospects. There are three kinds of people, if we consider the general motives that guide them. First are the self-sufficient who think and act for themselves and on their own motion. Second are those who need support, who want the approval of others for their thinking and acting or even want to take thought and action—and beliefs, too—ready-made. Third are those who live in a vacuum, who do not want to think or act at all, and whose beliefs are passive. The Communists cannot get the first kind and do not want the third. Their rank-and-file membership, therefore, is perforce drawn largely from the second.

Even here they are limited. Other factors must help to drive the recruit toward the party rather than toward some other more generally acceptable organization which will provide the desired guidance. That is why these stories in which the individual's altruism is so greatly stressed show underneath the influence of the home environment, of a romance, of some difficulty in adjusting to work or study or companions.

Some or all of these, plus the fact that they have the widespread and typically American urge to join something, are the factors that make them join the Communist party rather than the Elks or Rotary, the League of Women Voters or a study club, a new cult or a health organization. When they are bigots rather than believers, these are the factors which send them into the party rather than the Klan or some other group which appeals to intolerance. It also seems to be true that the party must rely for its hard core of unswerving members, spies, and saboteurs upon the bigots, although that hard core was not the subject of this study.

~~~~~~~~~~~~~~~~~~~~~~~~~~~~~~

CHAPTER EIGHT

DAMAGED SOULS

BEHIND the façade of idealism which communism erects for itself, and which is real enough in some cases, there is a tremendous amount of personal disappointment. The party would appear to be heavily populated with the handicapped—some of them physically, but more of them psychologically to a point that might be called emotionally crippling. They have borne a burden of frustration so heavy that it has become unbearable. In the Communist party they find a certain amount of relief, often temporary, but always welcome.

Communists themselves sometimes explain the relatively large number of weak, physically unattractive, or emotionally unstable members by saying these people have been freed by their suffering for serious study and so turn to communism. The more accurate explanation seems to be that they turn to communism because their handicap is neither so noticeable nor so much of an obstacle in the party as it has been in the world outside.

This does not mean that most or even very many Communists are candidates for some kind of an institution. Their psychological difficulties are seldom of a nature to incapacitate them for society, and their mental ability often is of a high order. Their physical defects are seldom disabling.

Among the emotionally upset, by far the larger group, there is often quite a complete unawareness of any psychological problem. They are attracted just because of this unawareness by the Communist theory of mental illness. The party preaches quite simply that the cause is the capitalist system; destroy the horrid competition, and the root of psychic sickness will be killed. This is very attractive to anyone whose own mind is a battleground of conflicts. It is much easier to work for the overthrow of capitalism than for the overthrow of an emotional conflict within oneself.

In general, these misfits who find or hope to find surcease in communism fall into one of several categories. These may be described briefly as:

1. The physically handicapped, whether by an obvious defect or a more than normal weakness of physique. Usually the defect is accompanied by some particularly bitter personal disappointments arising from it. Typical in our material is the case of one man who lost his leg in an accident while at work. His lawyer, while the victim was in hospital, "won" a settlement of $200 from the company. Only after he had signed the papers did the one-legged man discover that the lawyer also represented the company. Within a year of his discharge from the hospital, our man was a member of the Communist party.

2. The emotionally and socially rejected. In this group are the unattractive or unpopular members of handsome, well-liked families, the child whose parents, without being at all domineering or overpowering, had not time for him or seemed to prefer a brother or sister, the lonely but studious kids who grew up ostracized from their fellows often because of their own shyness and insecurity.

3. The guilty rich. Here is the explanation of the wealthy Communist, often inexplicable to the casual observer who thinks these people have benefited so greatly from the capitalist system that they are fools or fiends for turning against it. In fact, they have been harmed by their wealth rather than helped because they cannot rid themselves of a sense of sin. They seek to expiate it in the arms of the party which most energetically denounces the source of their material comforts and luxuries. It is much easier to do this than to obey the scriptural injunction about giving all to the poor. The party does not ask that. It allows the rich member to keep his capital, only contributing to party causes in full proportion to his income.

4. The resentful newly poor. It would appear that among the poor, Americans whose families once had comfortable incomes are the most likely recruits for communism. Men and women who have lived in poverty all their lives are sufficiently realistic to discount Communist propaganda.

Sophie K— represents three of these groups, all of them except the guilty rich. The fifth of six children of a Polish immigrant who had become a successful builder in Chicago, her earliest recollections are of the lamentations in the home over past glories. Mr. K— had been wiped out in the depression and was an intermittently employed laborer on the sort of jobs he had once financed himself. Mrs. K— did her housework resentfully, having had a taste of leisure but not for long enough to be bored by it. The children left home as soon as they could get jobs.

Polio had left Sophie with one leg slightly crippled, and this coupled with her long illness and family environment had made her painfully shy, frightened, and lonely. She never learned to play easily with other children.

"I think the prime reason for my joining the Communist party at the age of 20," she writes, "was the fact that I had no friends and was alienated from my family. I was just plain lonely and wanted to 'belong' somewhere. Romance had nothing to do with my joining. In fact, at the time I joined I was afraid of men and very virginal.

"All of my sisters were beautiful compared to me. My brothers were outstanding athletes at one time. One of my brothers who is now very successful was at one time a Communist."

This was the brother Sophie most admired, and it was hardly surprising that she should have followed him into the party, although apparently he did little to urge her. Once in, she found a whole new life opening before her. No one of her new associates seemed to mind the fact that she limped and was not pretty. None attempted wisecracks over her rather long Polish name. She warmed to the first real comradeship she had known, and was proud to work hard at volunteer typing jobs and to study everything that was recommended.

"I was repelled by the secrecy and could never manage to maintain the amount the party wanted me to maintain," she says. "But this experience in the party for nearly three years had a great influence on the development of my personality. I learned a great deal about the Negro and the history of the Negro people. I was influenced, too, by some of the speakers and writers."

Sophie left the party as a result of a Communist betrayal which may not have been unrelated to her unwillingness to live up to the code of secrecy. Perhaps she was caught in a crisscross of clashing personalities within the party. At any rate, the fact of her membership was revealed and she lost her job.

"My reaction is one of complete disillusionment and yet relief at being out of it," she says now. "I don't know

what I believe in really any more. I am afraid to get a job
and fearful of party blackmail."

Sophie's solitary life outside the party is even more bitter than the loneliness she had known before she joined.
She had tasted the joy of "belonging" and the delights of
friendship. Now she is afraid to belong to anything even if
she could. The only friends she ever had have united to
revile her or (which is worse) ignore her.

She has lost something else, the sense of trust in the
party which could do no wrong. To people like Sophie
there was a great relief in getting the answers to all problems, personal or impersonal, and to know the answers
were part of a great movement adhered to by the sort of
people one liked. Criticism was on a lofty scale for one's
own good, not a nagging to make one feel small. In fact,
as she saw it, most of the criticism was self-criticism, encouraged in order to make her a better party member. She
felt it constructive and helpful, never belittling or de-
grading.

In return for all this, Sophie was not at all averse to allowing her intelligence to abdicate when it came to appraising Communist leadership. She was quite willing to
take it for granted that Communist leaders were perfect
in every way. The fact that they were in Russia and never
seen made it easier to suppose them infallible. Even when
there was a shift in the party line or a replacement of
United States leadership, Sophie's background and experience enabled her to accept the change without protest.
Those who fail deserve to fail, she had decided. So there
was no sympathy for the fallen.

It is hard to say whether Daniel H— was turned toward
communism more by his early home environment or by
his difficulty in making friends. It would be even more
difficult to attempt to sort out these two influences one

from another. An only child, he was rather thoroughly and unhappily rejected.

"My parents were divorced when I was 16," he explains. "Both remarried almost immediately and each had another child by the second husband and wife soon after."

Daniel had no feeling of a place in either home after that, and when he was 18 and at college he joined the Communist party. Looking back at it, he says:

"Social pressure was the first reason for my joining; only secondarily was it political. Most of the people I wanted as friends were members. At that time, I believed communism to be the only answer to the world's problems, and I wanted to do my part. Because they were a well-disciplined organization, they filled social needs for people who felt rejected. The party also provided identification with a political cause. To people like me it was a chance to combat loneliness and satisfy social needs without having to admit to yourself that you were lonely and maladjusted; it was more dignified to think of joining for an ideal or a cause.

"I had some slight arguments about my membership with my family, for they knew of it, but nothing very serious. They were not extremists in their political views."

As so often happens with young people who join the party while at school or college, the Communist insistence upon study and perhaps the normal process of maturing brings about the break. At least that is what Daniel thinks now, for as he grew more familiar with the party's aims and methods, the less he liked them.

"The Stalin-Hitler pact was what got me out," he says.

He was then 20. It took him another year and a half to make the final break, and as might be expected he not only thought about it very carefully, for he had a strong "fear of social ostracism," but simply dropped away without explanation.

"I had not resigned," he explains, "but my friends in the party had reported that I was disagreeing with the party and had no intention of working for it. I had vague private fears that something might happen, but nothing ever did. Today I have contempt and fear of the damage the commies have done and what the USSR may still do."

A few months after Daniel H— dropped out of the party he took his degree. In his profession, teaching, he has been modestly successful. He has been married ten years and no longer fears either social ostracism or job discrimination. He was so inactive in the party, he explains, that it could not be held against him after all these years.

Sophie and Daniel demonstrate that it is not only the domineering father or the overwhelming mother who creates a home life which molds potential Communist recruits. The children of such parents, as has been noted, normally and healthily rebel against parental attitudes and in the rebellion sometimes drift to communism. At home they have been too much protected, too minutely guided. Children like Sophie and Daniel, whose souls are much more severely damaged, are more likely to suffer through family neglect or rejection. They are filled with frustrations and fears. They join the party as a refuge, where the others join out of defiance.

In a way, the desire to belong influences the wealthy who join the Communist party quite as much as the moderately well-to-do. In spite of their wealth, some rich folk have a positive disinclination to associate with others in the same income bracket. They are oppressed by a sense of guilt. They have been strongly influenced by the many dramatic books that have been written about the origin of the greatest American fortunes, and they suppose that it is impossible to achieve substantial wealth without fraud and injustice. They may have been disowned or at least distrusted by their parents for their radical views, or they may have broken away from home on their own initiative.

The Communist party has far fewer wealthy supporters than some other totalitarian movements in this country have been able to command. Some of those other movements seem to owe their big contributions to the wealthy giver's desire to hedge against the possible success of the movement. A Fascist group may and often does get large sums from individuals who would be ashamed to have their names associated with the movement. They "invest" just in case the movement might succeed. Then, they think, they would be safe.

It is doubtful whether the Communists get support for the same reasons as the Fascist bigots. Communism's millions come from other sources. Few men or women of great wealth would feel that they could be safe even if they did contribute, for they know that communism is not to be trusted. Even those who might want to buy safety would not think it possible. Of course those who think they buy Fascist favor are as mistaken as those who, merely for insurance, might contribute to a Communist cause without believing in it. The Fascist's record for betraying or liquidating financial supporters is even better known than that of the Communist's. Communism draws its wealthy supporters to it by conviction rather than fear.

There seem to be two kinds. One is the relatively young heir to a fortune who is ashamed of how he got his money and thinks he can make amends. The other is relatively elderly, usually a woman, who is drawn into communism by someone younger than herself and is glad to feel that she is devoting her ill-gotten or ill-inherited money to good works.

In the first group is most of the highly paid Hollywood and radio talent that was drawn into the party. In the stories told by each of them in public is some expression showing a feeling of guilt that he was making so much money while the world was in desperate plight. They wanted to escape the sense of sin their earnings gave them. In part this explains their choice of the Communist party rather than some other cause not so belligerently or at least vocally opposed to big salaries.

In the other group are the three economically secure, elderly women who for years were technically the owners of the *Daily Worker*, the Communist newspaper. They are from old and generally conservative American families, but they served for some years as the titular proprietors of a politically alien journal.

It is customary to suppose that women who have gone in for this sort of Communist support are akin to the well-meaning but rather impractical females who endow odd cults and fads. This is generally not so of the Communist. Most of these women have lived full and usually useful lives, eagerly sponsoring causes which they believe to be for the welfare of mankind. All three of the women who "owned" the *Daily Worker* were in this category.

Miss Ann M. W. Pennypacker, the youngest, was born in 1876, daughter of Samuel W. Pennypacker, who was governor of Pennsylvania from 1905 to 1909. She was a public-school nurse for 30 years. Mrs. Ferdinanda Weiselhoeft Reed, widow of a Unitarian minister-turned-schoolmaster, helps her daughter run a left-wing bookstore in California and has been associated with left-wing movements ever since she left college. She is six years older than

Miss Pennypacker. Mrs. Susan Homans Woodruff, two years older still, was a schoolteacher and lives in New York's Greenwich Village with her husband. All three of these women are well-to-do, strongly influenced by nineteenth-century philosophical radicalism, admirers of Soviet Russia, where all three have visited. They had no voice in the policy of the *Daily Worker* when they owned it. They were only its "guardian angels in time of crisis." This meant they helped the paper meet the capitalist requirement of stating the ownership. They were recruited, apparently not only for their respectability and old names but to avoid Congressional investigation. Few Congressmen would want to risk the ridicule they would face if they began to pry into the lives of three inoffensive old women.

Among the Communists with an emotional disturbance which amounts almost to mental disease are those who have become collectors of grievances and injustices. They are very much like those querulous, irritable people who in their own imaginations are always being put upon by others, who feel that the world is doing them untold wrongs and that everyone is out to cheat them. The Communist counterpart is admittedly not fearful of injustice to himself but rather to that vague collectivism which he calls the people.

This sort of Communist rejoices in every social wrong, becomes a collector of lynchings, wrongful imprisonments, arbitrary discharges, acts of discrimination. In some this disease is carried to the point of compulsive distortions. Of course it is not confined to Communists either. Thus when the late Heywood Broun, an avowed anti-Communist, wanted to get arrested to make a point about some wrong that he thought had been committed, and failed, he jumped into a patrol wagon to force the issue.

Most Communists prefer, as probably do the rest of us, to see the victim someone other than themselves. But a great many volunteer for sacrifice, eager to be arrested and jailed for the cause. They seem to be at least as much interested in satisfying their own peculiar need for punishment as they are in gaining publicity for the cause. They believe they are proving their worth to themselves and their fellows. This is emotionally related to the spirit which prompts youths to volunteer for especially hazardous duty in wartime. The war hero sometimes is sick emotionally, too. The exaggerated need to win the approval of one's fellows is a mark of mental illness. The outward act may be one of selfless devotion; the motive is what gives the thing away.

These people are like the hypochondriac who cherishes all his aches and pains and loves to tell people about them. The Communist often is a collector of social aches and pains and is much more enthusiastic about describing and deploring them than in doing something specific to correct them. Thus there is genuine joy among many Communists when a lynching is reported. Sympathy for the murdered man and his family is drowned by pleasure in the propaganda value of injustice. These particular Communists seem to be those who most enjoy the underground activities of the party, the spying on other members, the expulsion of a comrade found guilty of talking to a Trotskyite. They include the suspicious whose capacity to exaggerate or invoke grievances at times approaches the paranoid. They also are among the sadistic ones who most eagerly agree to the martyrdom of a comrade. For the party is not averse to sacrificing its own when the gain is deemed to be worth a little suffering—and a little gain is usually all that is required.

A lawyer was approached some years ago to represent the *Daily Worker* in a court case involving alleged obscenity. Four or five members of the staff were charged with the crime. In his opinion the case could have been won on its merits. But he would not take the case because the management of the party would not permit him to interview the individuals he was supposed to defend. The party wanted to decide which of them should go to jail without much defense, which ones should be spared, and which should be converted into martyr heroes. The leaders were much more eager to get a good point for their propaganda of the injustice of capitalism than they were to help establish the principle of freedom of the press. In any event the liberty of the individuals was considered totally irrelevant.

The lure that this emphasis on injustice can have for the damaged soul is exemplified in the story of Caroline J—, a young woman from the Middle West who took up secretarial work so she could get away from her well-to-do family, into which she had fitted rather unhappily. She had always felt a little out of things and lonely because her two elder sisters were better looking, better at school work, better at sports, and more popular, as well as being favored by their parents. She writes:

"I was 24 when I joined the Communist party in 1937 and was living in one of the Southern states. I was single and had been working for a large government enterprise for about a year, my first regular employment following graduation from college in 1935 and secretarial school in 1936.

"I joined the Communist party after having been employed one year. That year was an experience totally different from anything I had known previously. The agency with which I was connected was young and socially exciting. Its employees came from all parts of the country, many victims of the depression whose effects were still very much felt. On the national scene the numbers of unemployed were large, labor organizations involved few, and in the old-line craft unions and in the region where I was working the Negro was segregated and constantly exploited.

"On the international scene, the Republic of Spain was trying to maintain itself against the onslaught of a potential dictator, and sympathies for those upholding and defending the Loyalist cause were being aroused. Efforts to ban Japanese-made goods from local counters were infinitesimal but productive of modest response.

"For the first time, in this Southern community, I came to learn much more about how working people live, and through reading and discussions and observation what the odds were that they were up against. Locally the organization of textile workers was barely under way, and nationally the CIO had just been born."

All this was an experience which Caroline shared with millions of her generation. It was a background but hardly a reason for turning Communist. But in this town, for the first time in her life, she was sought after, asked to join committees and help organize lectures. She met other people besides the Communists, but a few members of the local union of government employees gave her the feeling of being wanted, which she never had enjoyed before.

"I slowly became a part of this group," she writes, "enjoyed being with them and taking part in what seemed like purposeful extracurricular activities—lecture series, educational foreign films sponsored by the union, workers' education committee of the union, central labor union attendance as union delegate, and later volunteer organizational work for the Textile Workers' Organizing Committee.

"It came as a surprise when I learned that the six or eight with whom I was most actively associating were members of the Communist party. That was my first knowledge that there was an organization of the party in the city. I wanted to continue being a member of this group of friends, wanted their approval. It wasn't long before I, too, accepted membership. The act of joining and the fact of membership seemed to give much more meaning to my life."

However, it is worth noting that for all her protestations of devotion to the cause, when the members of the group who had sought her out moved away from the city, Caroline moved out of the party. It is pleasant to be able to record, too, that she found another haven in marriage and children, relationships which provide her with all the sense of being wanted that she could ask.

These people whom we have chosen to call damaged souls have their counterparts in many who never have thought of joining the Communist party. Obviously the damage to the soul is not the entire reason for joining either. But these usually young men and women have one characteristic that is not so prominent in others who are equally unattractive or rejected or neglected. They are seeking to hide a flaw in themselves by dedicating themselves to correcting what they think are flaws in society.

Whether this has any therapeutic value for the individual we do not know. But it is not very beneficial to society. The net reforms accomplished by this sort of indirection are negligible.

It is significant that in the majority of cases, these members of the Communist party with whom we have talked left under one of two circumstances. Some gained an insight into the flaws in themselves, and the same insight led them to look more clearly at Communist aims and methods. The others discovered that the effort to remake the world did not relieve their fears and frustrations anyway.

~~~~~~

CHAPTER NINE

MINORITIES

ONE of the recurrent fears of many anti-Communists is that the party will capture one or several of the "minorities" in this country and use the group or groups as a revolutionary weapon to seize power. The minorities usually feared are the Negroes, the Jews, and the foreign-born. The fear seems to be based much more on the uncomfortable feeling that these groups are unfairly treated than on any success the Communist party has had in recruiting members among them.

All Americans belong to a minority of some kind—either national or local. But the ones that the Communists are supposed to be able to attract in substantial numbers are those minorities which have good reason to be dissatisfied with their standing in their communities. Of all of them, of course, the Negro has the most reason for complaint. Therefore, if the fears of those who think this makes Communists were justified, Negroes should provide more than their due proportion of the party members. In actual fact, they provide far fewer than this proportion. Communist leaders themselves frequently have bewailed their spectacular failure with the American Negro.

The minorities from which the greatest number of

rank-and-file card-holders are drawn—the ones we speak of in this book—are the minorities of the college-educated and of the upper-income brackets. In fact, a comprehensive study of the problem might well show that the small number of Negroes in the party is related to the poverty of the great majority of the Negro population. Jews and Catholics appear in what is perhaps more than their proportion of the population, but this appears to be due to the fact that the Communist membership is largely concentrated in large cities. This is where Jews and Catholics live, too. It is doubtful if these two groups are represented in the party in any greater numbers than their proportion of the large-city population.

The foreign-born are almost as infrequent among the rank-and-file members as Negroes, even though they are a majority of the leadership. This is because in the upper ranks of the party there is a highly disproportionate number of members born in Russia or the offspring of Russians. In view of the domination of the party by Moscow, this should hardly be surprising. The figures for 1948 were compiled by the FBI, and some of them are hitherto unpublished.

At that time there were 5,395 members of the party who were in positions of leadership. Of these only 411 were Negroes. This is a smaller percentage than the percentage of Negroes in the country. On the other hand, it is a very high percentage of all Negro Communist party members; about one fourth of the Negroes were classed as leaders. Of the remaining 4,984 the statistics show:

3,908 or 78.4% were foreign-born or with one or both parents foreign-born.

647 or 13% were married to persons of foreign stock.

429 or 8.6% were of native stock with native spouses.

If we deduct those of native stock with native spouses

we find that the 4,555 remaining Communists in positions of leadership stemmed mainly from Russia or her neighbors. The breakdown shows:

835 were born in Russia.

1,019 more had one or both parents born in Russia.

348 were married to persons of Russian stock.

370 were born in countries adjacent to Russia (Poland, Finland, Romania, Lithuania, Latvia, Turkey, Estonia).

190 more were born of one or both parents from these countries.

54 were married to persons of this stock.

897 were born in foreign countries other than those mentioned.

597 more had one or both parents born in these countries.

245 were married to persons of foreign stock other than Russia or neighboring countries.

Yet the great majority of the rank-and-file membership is native-born.

Nevertheless, the representation of minority groups, even though a minority within the party, is important if only because it is misinterpreted to indicate that communism is an outgrowth of these groups. It would appear that these people are attracted to the party very much on the same basis as others—the same psychological basis—and not very much because they are members of a minority with reason to be dissatisfied. The one exception to this statement is that insofar as their minority status has led them to feel frustrated and outcast, they derive the benefit of a sense of "belonging" when they take out their party cards.

Much of our own knowledge of the minority groups in the party came from those of our collaborators who themselves were not members of any groups generally regarded as minorities.

Of all the minorities in the United States who, by reason of discrimination and poverty, might be supposed to be fair game for Communist recruiting drives, the Negroes would seem to be by long odds the most likely. From time to time, the Communist party has made special efforts to enlist them, and at all times it has posed as the champion of equality and opportunity. As early as 1928 and intermittently thereafter, the Communist line called for establishment of an independent Negro Soviet Republic in what the party itself called the Black Belt. The idea was devised by Communists who had never seen the United States and had seen very few Negroes. They elaborated the idea in terms of the various republics of the Soviet Union, and apparently American Communists never were able to convince them that there might be fundamental differences between the problems and attitudes of American Negroes and Russian minorities.

The propaganda for a Negro Soviet Republic was singularly unappealing to American Negroes. Negro Communists themselves hoped for better results through agitation for equal rights and opportunities, which are the obvious desires of their race in this country. Two recent books on the subject—*Communism Versus the Negro* by William A. Nolan and *The Negro and the Communist Party* by Wilson Record—show how all the Communist programs failed to enlist any large number of Negroes. Mr. Nolan, after an exhaustive study of the available facts, reports that the peak Negro membership was claimed in 1939, when the figure was put at 5,005. He notes that the Pittsburgh *Courier,* a leading Negro newspaper, reported a year later that there were only 250 of these 5,005 left in the party and only 50 of them paid dues. Mr. Nolan reports a finding by an investigator for the Un-American Affairs Committee (a committee not usually inclined to minimize the Communist menace) that in 1949 there were only 1,400 Negroes in the party. This figure is very close to that of others who have studied the facts available.

Coming from the statistical general to the individual, the story of Albert N— explains much of the Communist technique, and the Communist failure, with Negroes. Albert is the oldest of five children reared in New York City. He was graduated from high school in the mid-thirties and went to work as an elevator operator in mid-Manhattan. He has put five years of army service and two marriages between his present situation and his Communist youth, and he writes:

"I come from a normal Negro family. Dad is and has been a postman for 28 years. He is and has been an ardent Democrat for as far back as my memory goes. He is a bug on education, a fair conversationalist, considers himself 'a race man,' and is a competent steady worker. He worked two jobs to send one daughter through college and the other as far as she cared to go through college. Dad has taken one too many from time to time through the years, enough to have caused my mother—Mudge to me—some embarrassment, but not enough to be considered a drunkard or even a really heavy drinker.

"Mother is an average Negro housewife, a bit prim and old-fashioned about some things, but seems endowed with that great understanding and tenderness which permits some women to mother their own children and most of their friends and neighbors as well. Mother is an excellent seamstress and during hard times has helped Dad shoulder the financial burden of the family. Mudge is the finest person I know—an opinion shared by many who are not fortunate enough to be her son.

"I joined the Young Communist League either in gratitude for their help in getting me into a CCC camp, or in an attempt to help me get there. I don't recall precisely which of the two was the motivating reason. Dad earned about $2,100 at that time. As the oldest son and only other working member of the household, I earned about $15 to $20 weekly. I was then about 19 years old.

"I was in the Y.C.L. about 14 months more or less. I attended most meetings, helped sell penny, nickel, and dime leaflets when it was my turn and helped union picketing on 14th Street. Both family and friends knew I was a member. There was no secrecy that I recall during those years.

"I do not remember or know of any individual or group of Communist speakers who made any genuine impression on my conscious thinking. I added a few words to my vocabulary and had a slightly increased interest in national politics and race relations. The Communists in those days probably pointed up the inequities of our democracy as concerned minority racial groups—I am thinking of the Negro especially.

"I think that most people join in order to have an emotional or creative outlet. The low-income-level non-intellectuals are able to forget some of their own troubles by making them mass troubles and fighting them on the class level. Their ranting and raving about these problems at Communist meetings give them an emotional outlet. The intellectuals and pseudo-intellectuals join because they haven't the intellect, talent, or training to become authors, musicians, artists, etc. Consequently they submerge their personality into or associate it with the whole

Communist effort to make an impression on the national and perhaps the international scene.

"I left, or rather didn't join, the Communist party because of the tiresome intensity of Communists themselves. I was too old to remain in the Y.C.L. Members of the party seemed overly serious about everything for my tastes, so in spite of efforts on their behalf, I did not join. I merely stopped attending meetings. Most of my friends were not Y.C.L.ers, but I did find that those in the Y.C.L. drifted away rapidly. There was no effect upon my family relationships, although Dad was happy about it. My life was about the same as before until three years ago when I was forced to resign from the Post Office because of my one-time Y.C.L. membership. Since then I have had to revise my living standards. I resigned after getting permission to have a hearing from the Post Office Loyalty Board. I have found it impossible to get a good job since then, and have had difficulty keeping *any* kind of job.

"Up until the last few years, I had been neither pro-Communist nor anti-Communist, mainly because of a failure to recognize communism as a Stalin-dictated world movement. I am now anti-Communist.

"I am less completely individualistic than prior to my Y.C.L. days. What little exposure I had to Communist theory made only one real impression on me. It can be summed up in one word: Organization. Not necessarily organization into trade unions, tenant leagues, and such, but organization in everything, that is, for example, household budgeting, letter writing, allocation of time for hobbies, recreation, etc."

Albert is typical of many former Communists of his race who were helped or thought they were helped to get a desired job by joining a Communist movement. This is much more true of them than of others, and yet the lure of a job has not been enough to hold them, nor enough to entice more than a handful of their fellows in the first place. Moreover, the lure of irregular hours—a Bohemian life—fails to attract the Latin, Negro, and other gayer social groups who have this freedom at home. It appeals more to those who were reared in the rigid New England or strictly religious Southern household.

As Mr. Record points out in his book, American Negroes never have been swept into radical movements in masses. They have gone to Communist meetings with pleasure, especially in the North, but they have been attracted principally by the hope of improvement, and have not been convinced that they can get it through the party. They seem to be more impressed by the realities of Communist tactics than by the avowed principles or talk of equality or even the reality of sexual equality and freedom. While there are whites, especially in the South, who think the Negro's greatest desire is sexual equality with whites, this actually rates last among the "rights" which Negroes themselves want. They put equality on the job, in housing, and in education far ahead.

Observers like Record and Nolan believe that much of the Communist party's patronizing attitudes toward the Negro is due to its foreign leadership. In any case, Negroes themselves seem to realize that in a Communist world, even in a Negro Soviet Republic, they would be subordinate to white commissars. The fact that some Communists in top positions are Negroes does not influence or fool the mass of their fellows very much. They have no respect for the Negro Communists as leaders of the race, whatever leadership these may exercise in the party.

The average Negro is more impressed by what actually happens than by words. Cases such as that of Irwin and Ruth V. are widely known and stick in Negro memories.

Irwin was a Negro who had managed a college education and while a student in North Carolina joined a cell of the Communist party. There he met and married Ruth, a white girl whose adherence to the party may not have been unrelated to her reaction from the violent anti-Negro attitude of her Southern parents and her love for her childhood nurse. Both Irwin and Ruth were from more than averagely prosperous families, and they may well have felt themselves in the vanguard of freedom and equality when they married.

At this point the party decided that expediency dictated a Jim Crowing of its operations in this state. The organization was broken into two cells. The leaders ordered Irwin to join the Negro cell while Ruth was to remain in the one for whites. The result was that both left the party.

It may well be that the sexual relationships between whites and Negroes seem much more proof of no discrimination to whites than to Negroes. While the sex play which communism uses as a part of propaganda acts as a symbol as well as a high stimulant in an erotic way, it seems to be far more impressive to the disapproving Southern white than to the Negro looking for justice in employment, in education, in housing, sanitation, health, and all the other common forms of living. To the educated, ambitious Negro, an opportunity for sexual intercourse is small compensation for discrimination on the job.

The fact that Negro Communists, like their white comrades, are by and large more highly educated and capable of higher earnings than the average seems partly to be the result of party policy. There has been little consistent effort to recruit the masses of Southern Negroes. The party apparently did not want great numbers of poverty-stricken, illiterate, or semiliterate men and women who would not pay dues, would be almost impossible to discipline, and would be of small use to the movement. Moreover, membership is closely related to good work habits, and the party wanted only members who had or obviously could acquire them. The result is that even despite job difficulties because of past Communist affiliation, not a single Negro we interviewed earned less than $3,000 a year—well above the racial average. Some at least of the Communist leaders knew quite well that in many parts of the South, great numbers of Negroes would sign anything a white man asked them to sign. They would be flattered by the request and also quite unaware of what they were signing.

Communists, therefore, sought for potential leaders—and by and large failed to get them. Most of those whom the party wanted in its ranks refused to exchange what they recognized was a status as second-class citizens in a free country for the promise of first-class citizenship in a Soviet dictatorship. The disillusionment of those who did join seems in general to have come even more rapidly for the Negro than for the young white boy or girl who was attracted to the party. Also the Negro seems to have enjoyed the secrecy and deception more. Otherwise, their stories are very much like those of white ex-Communists.

Grover S— is a fairly recent convert from communism. He says:

"I am a Negro with practically no education. My family had lived in the South and there were lots of kids, and none of us had a chance. I ran away from home at the age of 16 and bummed my way to Chicago. I had very little to do with my brothers and sisters since I left the South.

"I got a job as a day laborer and happened to be working alongside a guy who had gone through high school and read magazines and books. This guy got me to do some reading. A union was formed and I joined. I found I was quite a talker, and although I did not know anything about the labor movement, I wanted more dough. After a year or two, I was shifted from outside trench work into the factory and finally got a job on a machine. Through the work of the union, I got about $1.10 an hour. It sounds like a lot of money, but we only worked about 35 weeks a year.

"The union was run by one man who took a shine to me. It turned out that he was a Communist, and he got me into the Communist party. I did not know what the hell it was all about. I did not understand what they were talking about, and even after I read their pamphlets, all I knew was that the union was Communist-run and the union was always fighting for more wages. Of course the union was Jim Crow, and I had trouble because after I left the trench work, most of the men at the machines were white. I never was active in the union of the men at the machines. I was popular in the laborer's union and became an officer. I joined a cell of the Communist party thinking it was only part of the union work.

"I was very lonely and made no friends except this one man who got me into the union. I had a lot of time on my hands, and I used to do a lot of union Communist party work. It was tough going getting Negroes into the union. They did not understand and they did not care, but they liked to hear Communist speakers because they always talked about the freeing of the Negroes. They told us that everybody in Russia loved Negroes.

"During this time I heard from my mother once in a while, but not until last year [after he had left the party] did I have any real contact with her. Incidentally, I am pretty good at music, although I never took a lesson.

"I liked the secret meetings of the cell, but what I enjoyed best was an order to do some job like distributing bundles of pamphlets or getting placards ready for the picket lines.

"I liked fun, and I now know that I missed all the fun while I was in the Communist party. They are damn serious people, and outside of a few wild sex parties, I never did anything to help the revolution.

"I got out of the party when I fell in love with a girl I picked up on a bus. She was working as a secretary in one of the big Negro anti-Communist organizations. I finally broke down and told her I had been a member of the Communist party. I trusted her that she would not squeal, but she said she would have nothing more to do with me unless I quit. I did quit. I was afraid to quit for a time because I know that the Communists raise hell with people who leave the party and they threatened and sometimes actually did send secret letters to bosses telling them that people were formerly Communists. I knew my way around enough that I felt that this would mean I could never get a job and hold it. Bosses don't hire Negroes very much and they certainly don't hire Negroes who were once Communists.

"My girl was really in love with me, and we talked it over for months, and she loved me enough to get a transfer to another city. We got married.

"This whole story, which sounds like a lot, lasted about four years because I am now 25. Incidentally, I was turned down for the army. The marriage is working out swell, and I have nothing to do with the Communists. I am getting interested in the NAACP [National Association for the Advancement of Colored People].

"I must say that the Negroes in my cell were all damn good workers and none were making less than 90 cents an hour. [This was considerably above the average for Negroes in that place.] The thing that I remember is that none of the dumbest of the Negroes would join the Communist party."

The fact that these "dumbest" members of his race were not attracted by communism surprised Grover, and perhaps pleased him since he could consider himself one of an elite group. But perhaps the reason was not their "dumbness."

Communists have not, according to former Negro members, done more than pay lip-service to the chief aspirations of the Negro people of this country. Mr. Nolan has pointed out that so long as the welfare of the Soviet Union comes first in the Communist world, it will be impossible for the party in this country to make the cause of Negroes its own. That is why, with this minority as with others, the membership attracts a few for various psychological reasons which have little to do with its ideology. The fact that the few were Negroes was a coincidence.

Communism among the Jews, Catholics, and foreign-born—of whom of course very many are Jews and Catholics —is a somewhat different story. As has been said, the foreign-born are mostly notable among the Communist leaders, not the rank and file. We have seen in previous chapters the reasons why some Jews and Catholics turned to and away from the Communist party. Among Catholics, the reason seldom had anything to do with their minority status. Usually they had more personal reasons, with revolt from one fount of authority leading them to put their trust in another institution which claimed infallibility. Sometimes Jewish Communists seem to have been influenced in joining the party to an extent because of a feeling of discrimination or of failing to belong to a desired group. However, it should be noted that both Catholics and Jews usually begin to be interested in communism only after they have fallen away from church or synagogue completely.

The canard that Jews dominate the Communist movement has been repeated and disproven at frequent intervals ever since the success of the Russian Revolution of 1917. It does seem to be true that in America Jews more than Negroes are inclined to put some faith in Communist professions of nondiscrimination. Actually, of course, they were confused by the Russian campaign to abolish religion —in itself a new bigotry. Russia had been for years notorious as the land of pogroms. Russian Jews, fleeing from persecution before World War I, were astounded to find anti-Semitism even if not the bloodiest style of pogrom in this country. Therefore, to the descendants of these immigrants, it seemed a wonderful mark of nondiscrimination when the revolution of 1917 put an end to pogroms. What they did not realize was that Jews in Russia now were persecuted not for their so-called race but for their adherence to a religion. Nondiscrimination consisted of this: A pious Jew was punished in the same way as a pious Christian.

So far as communism is still Marxist, it is also anti-Semitic, for there is considerable evidence of this in Marx himself. As a more modern example of the Communist attitude, Russia and her satellites have been busily removing Jews from positions of party or government responsibility.

Nevertheless, all this was seldom known to American Jews who were lukewarm or lacking in religious belief. Those who had been hurt by discrimination furthermore did not find in the party any obvious contradiction of the proclaimed tolerance, as Negroes did. Even among these, however, the frustrations caused by minority status seem to be subordinate to other psychological factors.

Leon C. seems to have been representative of many American Jews in this as in other respects. His father had been a good provider, certainly in the middle income group, until he died when Leon had completed his first year of high school. The boy was obliged to go to work at once. But he put himself through high school and completed three years of college work by studying at night. He became a writer and editor, and as the 1930's were tolling the knell of the good old ways and days, he became more and more attracted to Communist philosophy. Of the party he says:

"It was the only group that appeared to be combating the rise of fascism in the world."

Leon was then 27, and like many other Jews saw in the anti-Semitism of the Nazis a personal as well as social threat. The anti-Semitism or rather the anti-Judaism of the Soviet regime never intruded upon his consciousness. In the party he worked on the editorial staff of a Communist magazine, and within four months began to feel disillusioned.

"I realized very soon that joining was a great mistake," he reports. "I found the atmosphere of secrecy and rule from the top intolerable, especially in light of the hypocritical pretenses. I found the party propaganda curiously ineffective; I never was really persuaded. I learned more about the party's operations, and the more I learned the more powerfully I opposed it."

In less than a year from the time he joined, he left, telling his friends and family that he was through with the party. He feels that he was not a member long enough to damage himself seriously, and yet:

"I feel barred from certain kinds of jobs, especially government employment. Probably my membership was a detriment during military service."

At the same time Leon is doing better financially in his

profession than he did during the brief period of his party membership. He is married and does not believe that his experience has damaged him in relation either to his wife or his children. It was an unhappy episode in his life, and he thinks he has put it behind him.

Monroe C—'s bitterness seems to have stemmed from the fact that although he had tried to throw off all traces of his Jewish background, even to the point of changing his name, he felt himself pursued by anti-Semitism. His father, a minor pillar of the Jewish community, had died when Monroe was quite young. His mother had remained active in Jewish women's organization.

The slights which the youth had suffered were small— jibes from schoolfellows, failing to be invited to join a college fraternity, being left out of invitations to parties. At one time he had thought he would like to be a doctor and was told Jews had a hard time getting into the medical colleges.

"I used to think it was unfair because I did not regard myself as a Jew," he said. "Then I found that the crowd considered left-wing at college didn't care. The ones who treated me the best turned out to be Communists, and I just sort of drifted into the party.

"I was pretty scornful of all organized religion, and the Communists seemed to have the right line on that. I thought their agitation would help bring on the day when religion would be outmoded and phony distinctions would be forgotten.

"I was in the party about a year. It was only after I got out that I began to realize that the Communist talk against discrimination was just talk. At the time, the regimentation of thought drove me out. If I wasn't going to take so-called divine words as gospel if they didn't make sense to me,

I certainly wasn't going to accept the dogmas of other men."

When young people have broken away from Catholicism, as Monroe did from Judaism, there does not seem to be much repining over a supposed minority status. But in some of these who contributed to this book, the effects of Catholic upbringing seemed to have left some traces, as one would expect. For example, John N. who was a party member in his twenties began his account of his experiences with:

"Possibly my story will be of help because I view those years of early manhood with regret but without guilt."

When he was discussing the difficulties of getting out of the party, he said:

"As long as membership is viewed as an almost irredeemable sin we make it difficult for people to say 'Peccavi.' To be sure, a few have been able to sell their peccavis at market—a market created by the daily press and magazines which encourage our people to enjoy an emotion which might be likened to that of the Roman crowds who watched Christians thrown to the lions. That leading Catholic laymen in our Congress assume positions of extreme unforgiveness is hard to understand, since of all the organized groups in our society that apparently understand the frailties of mankind, the Catholics in general have thus far appeared to be the most humane."

John was drawn into the party actually by the combination of secret rebellion against a father who dominated his family without realizing the impact of his own personality, and of falling in love with a Communist girl, who also had ceased to profess Catholicism, in which she had been reared. This combination is common, but it is perhaps significant that John was surprised that the girl "did not feel guilty" about leaving the church. He explains, perhaps more to himself than to us:

"Coming from New Orleans, she was not like our North-eastern Catholic members; she wasn't Irish as I was by inheritance, and she wasn't Puritan in her fears and hypocrisies."

Even less important than the effects of early Catholic training, at least among those we are considering, is the influence of foreign birth or foreign parentage. Most of those who gave us their life stories obviously had been affected by growing up in a home alien to the life they found outside the home. But it does not seem to have been in any way different from the great majority of the foreign-born who have never been remotely attracted to communism. We see this minority influence operating only through a more determined, conscious rebellion against parental authority.

Among the foreign-born Communist rank-and-file members we saw or heard from, very few had been active in organizations of the national group from which they sprang. In fact, both before, during, and after their membership, they seemed to scorn the men and women who kept up the foreign language, belonged to a society of Italians or Poles or Germans or whatever the nationality may have been.

Would these racial, religious, and national minority representatives have been Communists anyway, given their family and social background? Leon, Monroe, John, and the rest do not know, and certainly it is impossible for anyone else to dogmatize about the point. It does appear to be true that when Negroes or aliens, Jews or Catholics join the Communist party, outsiders are the ones who make the most of the racial or religious background, whereas they would not think of looking for a motive of this kind among native-born whites who were raised as Protestants. Yet the great majority of the rank and file consists of these native-born Protestant whites.

It would appear, therefore, that the groups usually considered as "minorities" in this country are also minorities among the Communist rank and file. Perhaps one reason is that many of the most minority-conscious individuals in our society generally are crusaders who want to improve the lot of their fellow religionists or nationals or racial group. Crusaders are single-minded people; crusaders for the rights of a minority want to concentrate on those rights and not on the broad, world-wide, and unpredictable program of communism. Often it has been pointed out that communism is directly opposed both to Zionism and religion, which command the ardent support of many Jews in this country. Negroes who fight for the rights of their race seldom wish to dissipate their energies on international revolution even supposing that they would be sympathetic to the principle, which most of them are not.

The Communist soon learns, as one of our collaborators put it in an aside while telling his personal story, that "bigotry is the party's best-selling card in the U.S.A. This even though the Kremlin would no doubt order the murder of every American Negro if such a step were needed to mount to power." But the man who said this belonged to no minority group which is the target for bigots. Intolerance is more effective in driving into the Communist party the members of the majority who resent bigotry than in recruiting the people who have something to fear from the bigots.

Dissatisfaction with minority status, then, seems to be much less important in the molding of a Communist than the rejection by or hostility to parents, the influence of a

sexual partner, the frustrations arising from a physical
or emotional handicap, or even the mistaken ardors of
youth. The desire for affection is primitive and natural.
Absence of the feeling of security which affection and
warmth usually bestow on a person can stem from group
or social as well as family or school isolation of course. So
the chief reason why minority status may sometimes play
a part in turning a minority-group member to communism
is the dislike and distrust which it generates in the family
and other personal relationships.

~~~~~~~~~~~~~~~~~~~~~~~~~~~~~~~~

CHAPTER TEN

SEX PATTERNS

BEFORE very many people in this country worried about the morals of Communists in the matter of espionage, there was a widespread interest in their morals sexually. It was extensively reported and often believed that life in the Communist party was one long sexual orgy. At one time there were probably more Americans who thought all Communists practiced "free love" and promiscuity than knew the name of Lenin.

The facts do not seem to be nearly so lurid, but are rather more enlightening. For sex is one of the mainsprings of a Communist's motivations just as it is for everyone else. This is true no matter what the actual sex life of an individual may be. Even if there is no sex life in the usual sense at all, it is true, perhaps under these rare circumstances especially true.

To be able to define a peculiarly Communist pattern of sexual behavior would require more study than we had either the resources or the talent to conduct. Perhaps we will know more about it as the monumental research being carried out by Professor Alfred C. Kinsey and his associates progresses. On the basis of our own inquiries we are willing to make these informed guesses as to what, in general, a full research job may uncover about our American Communists:

1. That their sex life is casual, rather random, somewhat less monogamous than the average of their income and education in the country, and also less sentimental or even intimate. The men would be more inclined to take their sex activity in the light of a form of calisthenics, and much of the male aggressiveness which in our society is often directed toward sex relations is drained off by party activities. The party frowns upon excessive intimacy, even in marriage, for there must be no competition in a member's life with the welfare of the party itself. Tenderness for a sexual partner might diminish the profound devotion which must be reserved for Stalin and Russia. At the same time, the party today frowns on casual sex relationships and encourages monogamy.

2. The matter-of-fact attitude toward sex is in part a declaration of independence from the morals of bourgeois society. The Communist wishes to prove himself or herself above the standard of sexual morality which his fellow citizens profess—and which, as Kinsey has shown, they rather seldom follow. Thus the Communist's extramarital sex relations may be no greater in number or extent than that of the average conservative of his own general background, but the Communist feels less guilt.

3. That the women members of the party were, as girls, more timid than the average and especially more scared of boys.

4. That a sexual attraction for a member of the opposite sex often is involved in the decision of a youngster to join the party—and a similar attraction even more frequently is involved in the decision to get out. This seems to be true of both sexes. It has been indicated in many of the histories already cited in this book, and will be seen in

more. An especially pointed example was a now highly respected lawyer who recently told one of us that he could not persuade a certain girl to go to bed with him unless he joined the patry. Did she afterward? Yes, he said, but it was not all he had dreamed and he left both the girl and the party in two months. Apparently the girl's reluctance to sleep with him before he was a party member was due to the Communist strictures on any such intimacy with outsiders. For the same reason, the party frowns on "mixed" marriages almost as sternly as the Catholic and Jewish orthodox churches.

5. That the casual acceptance of sex is related to the similar attitude toward marriage and divorce. Both these institutions are bent to the party line. Marriage—and Communists seem to have more than their proportion of common-law marriages, since to some of the converts from bourgeois homes emancipation means freedom from formal wedlock—is sanctioned so long as the partner is a party member or at least fully sympathetic. A split in loyalty to the party frequently is the cause of a split in marriage, or vice versa—at least the two are often coincidental. Divorce is irrelevant except as it affects the party. Thus prominent party members ask permission of headquarters to get a divorce. The fact that they see the necessity for asking indicates the party's power over the romantic and sexual life of members.

6. That celibacy is virtually nonexistent, and that there is not the degree of impotence among the men which, according to the Kinsey statistics for the general population, we should expect to find.

7. That the party members are more prudish in speech and outward manner than the average of their education in this country. The language at a Communist social event is less pornographic and members are less inclined toward

the smoking-room anecdote. We would guess that a survey of the drawings and writings on the toilet walls at Communist headquarters would reveal few romantic symbols on the women's side and few erotic or pornographic scrawls on the men's. That is, few in comparison with the washrooms of the rest of the country, whether in swank hotel or roadside diner.

8. That there is a reasonable (from the standpoint of the Kinsey findings) quota of homosexual or suppressed homosexual personalities. In fact, there are some psychoanalysts who say that there is a slight analogy between the analysis of a Communist and that of a homosexual. These analysts explain that among both they find individuals who want their shame and enjoy the guilt of lying, cheating, and deceiving their friends. Complacency over guilt may reduce the sense of responsibility. This theory probably would not meet the approval of other analysts.

9. That jealousy is less prevalent, a feature which would be expected in view of the general attitude toward sex. It is also partly attributable to the fact that casual relationships, even within marriage and monogamy, are sufficiently pleasing to the members. If there is any trouble, the troubled one can throw himself into his work and forget any jealous pangs.

10. That there is less recourse to prostitutes among party members than among non-Communists of the same age, background, and marital status. Especially in an underground movement promiscuity would be frowned upon because of the obvious dangers of divulging secrets, and the same thing is true of casual amours. The party is well aware of the lure of a pretty girl or a virile man, and while it does not use the lure as much as fiction would have it (perhaps because the party does not command enough of the raw material), it does not want its own members

seduced. The party's interest in the sexual lives of members is shown by the fact that its 1951 loyalty checks inquire closely into all sexual activities, with a special question on prostitutes. However, we suggest that the Communist's avoidance of prostitutes has a deeper emotional reason than party disapproval.

Looking back, a great many former Communists recognize the part that their sexual development played in both their entrance into the party and their exits. Like every other factor, it is only part of the story and must be related to the rest if the whole is to be understood.

Edna E. was a product of the South which looks backward rather than forward. She was brought up on a large plantation with much service, great pride, and not very much cash. The family was not a very stable environment. Edna thinks that she had grown up with an admiration for her father, who "ran out on Mother," and an active hostility to her mother. Her upbringing was, as she puts it "very feminine, à la South." Her schooling came to an end after one year of college. By that time an older sister had been married and divorced. Edna does not think she was politically aware any more than she was interested in sports or scholarship.

"I was concerned about the KKK in the South," she says. "A school friend was a member as a kid."

This concern had little to do with her membership in the Communist party. For that she was indebted to a youth a year older than herself who came from the North. She was 19 and was going to leave home and become a stenographer.

"He was my first love," she explained. "I was n.g. at the start, and he aroused me for a time."

The young man joined the party, and she followed him into it. They lived together for several years, and without any of the amenities of service to which Edna had been accustomed at home. Also without some of the prejudices. She recalls:

"I was active on a very low level of the party. They wanted me to mix with Negroes, to educate me. It did just that. I became a fair stenographer. The whole experience was of great value. I learned much, too much, but I learned how to work hard and long hours. I learned to be a sneak, but I loved the secrecy."

All this was early in the United States participation in World War II, and Edna remained in the party until after the end of the war. But for the last year she was in the process of getting out. What was her motive?

"Mainly a new lover, non-CP. I hope to marry him. I left my first lover when he played around in CP fashion with all the girls. Remember, sex is different for CP than for others. No romanticism or sentimentality is permitted. You are a bride of Stalin!"

For all that she had decided to leave the party, Edna hesitated. Her membership had been a secret from her family, and her relations with them were unhappy. She was also scared of her comrades, saying:

"They stop at nothing. I crucified several ex-CPers and so I knew what they would do to me—tell my mother, my boss, etc. The press helps the party in this. If the press changed, particularly Hearst, the party would have to relax."

Edna finally got out quietly by the expedient of moving to another city. She thinks she has come to believe more than she did in "honesty and morality." She also finds it pleasant to be making decisions for herself "but my boy friend is needed at times."

The male counterpart of Edna is Edward C—. He, too, was brought up in a home of many servants, but his family had cash, too. His father, a manufacturer in New England, was a stern man who expected his son to take his ideas as well as his career from Papa. The ideas were those of the right-wing Republican to whom the depression taught nothing. The career, manufacturing, repelled his son but the boy did not dare say so. It is doubtful if the elder C— ever knew that his son was a rebel, and apparently the son did not know it either for a long time. He writes outlining these facts, and adds:

"My sexual education was delayed intellectually and emotionally. But I ran into a girl while I was at college who was the first person who, looking back, had talked to me about social causes. She also came from a well-to-do background, but while at college was active in studying about labor unions and working in youth movements in the fight against bigotry. Our family was high Episcopalian. Because of our name we were always thought to be Irish Catholics.

"I fell in love with this girl, and she educated me intellectually and sexually."

Apparently it was the courage which this experience gave him that prompted him to tell his father that he did not propose to be a manufacturer and would if necessary stand on his own feet. He explains:

"I had an independent income from my grandfather's will and although it was not big, I had felt that I could always live on this $4,000 a year, which was fairly well secured. I lived with this girl friend for some years and when I was graduated married her. Although I had been brought up in a swank suburb, after I got married I lived in a working-class district.

"At the time I took up with my wife, she was pretty far left, although neither she nor I knew much about left, right, or center. We both became increasingly active in young people's organizations, and she finally told me that she had decided to join the Communist party. I went along with her and although I enjoyed the secrecy of meetings, alibis, code names, and the rest of the rigmarole, she was always much more mature and would not fall for this stuff.

"My wife and I lived happily and modestly while in the party and followed national and international events with great care. I should imagine that more words are read every day by the members of the Communist party than by any other group in the United States, including possibly even by faculties of colleges. I have probably read more than my wife did because I was less social and found it less fun to be with a group of friends.

"While in the party, I adopted the party attitude toward sex; communism cannot thrive if personal attachments are really strong. There must be only one personal attachment, and that is to the movement. Looking back at it, I must say it is too bad that other organizations cannot evoke the same degree of dedication and selflessness and sacrifices. The meetings at Madison Square Garden were thrilling, and I do suggest that the Republicans and Democrats might well have looked at some of those meetings to learn what can be done to put on a big show to step up people's emotions.

"In the course of our emotional ramblings, my wife at one time thought she was in love with another man. This came as a great jar to me and we had some terrible emotional scenes. I tried the usual stuff of seeking to make her jealous and finally realized I was deeply devoted to her. In the course of her breaking away from her romance with what happened to be a non-Communist, we were brought closer together, and exactly to the degree that we got closer together, our adherence to the party diminished. As we cooled—and I think cooled is a good word in this sense—

our eyes were opened to a new appraisal of the movement. Having broken through the emotional monopoly which is claimed for Papa Stalin, we gradually were able to break through the intellectual monopoly. I mean by this we started to read with some critical judgment arguments against Communist positions. Instead of thinking Dubinsky, for example, was a labor devil, we became impressed with his argument that Communists were destroying the labor movement and that Communists did not want a labor movement except for the purpose of capturing it in order to capture the government of the United States.

"My next problem was how to get out of the movement. Being minor cogs in the machine, we were able to drift away gradually. Of course we had to lie on many occasions and repeatedly make excuses for nonattendance at meetings and then for nonpayment of assessments and dues. (Incidentally, isn't it surprising that these stupid Congressmen have never brought out the facts in regard to the vast wealth gathered by the party each year in the United States?)

"In connection with getting out, we had to be very careful because by this time I had a job in a manufacturing business, not my father's, and I know that the company would have fired me if they had known that I had been a member. This, even though the product we made had no relation to the military requirements of our government. Night after night we considered how we should move against the potential threat of blackmail held by the party. They write anonymous letters to the employer, identifying ex-members in order to have them fired. In this respect they are really as bad as McCarthy. If we had had any information of real value, we would have gone to the FBI. In the absence of such information, we did not go because we had been brought up in decent homes and we were taught not to squeal on anyone. Incidentally, I have yet to see some good writing on this ethical problem. Moreover, we had become friendly and felt close to other young people in the party, and you do not readily squeal on or get into trouble someone to whom you have been close. Of course the Communists play on this tradition in American life. They have specific instructions for making life miserable for ex-members. Of course, if you really think that you are going to save mankind, such deviations from our code of decency are easily overlooked. Throughout history, crusaders were never reluctant to kill if necessary to accomplish the objects of the crusade.

"Our family is in good shape. We have joined liberal, democratic movements. We are active in the Liberal party in New York City, as are so many ex-Communists. In a few years I will be making $15,000 a year. We have kept our tastes simple and as a matter of fact, the accumulation of money has never been accented. We learned much in the party in the way of diligence and sacrifice, but now we seem to be grown up; at least we enjoy making our own decisions. We take orders from no one, and if we are outvoted in any organization of which we are members, we accept our minority position as proper in the democratic process."

Perhaps some indication of how the drift to betrayal can come about is to be seen in the distraught confession of Sarah R., who was trying to make the grade as a Communist. A simple and hard-working girl of good, almost smart appearance, she was caught smuggling out copies of letters written by her employer.

"I was working for an investment banking house and copied letters sent out by partners in the firm," she writes. "I was 20 years old and I was in love with a top official of the Young Communist movement."

The young man, a war veteran and very glamorous to Sarah, told her that she was living in a capitalist world and had to prove herself before she could be trusted to change it. If she was good enough at jobs like copying confidential letters from leading industrialists, she might get into the Communist party, he explained. Sarah could only think of how much she was in love. But after she was caught she wrote:

"I come from a middle-class Jewish family, and I would die rather than have my folks know that I had copied firm letters and sent them to the Communist organization. But I won't give up my beau. I signed a confession and I said I knew it was not the right thing to do, but I consoled myself with the thought that the letters I copied came through the mailbox and therefore were not so personal in nature.

"If I could only make you believe that it was the first time that I had ever done anything as sneaky as that, and that I had never done anything that was considered disloyal to the firm! I never cheated nor stole nor had been a sneak. I am sorry that at this date I had no thought of loyalty or disloyalty, but I promise never to do anything of that low caliber again."

It is hard to believe after talking to Sarah that if she had had a love affair with the average youth—for she would never have been attracted by the more obvious forms of dishonesty—she could have run so counter to her upbringing.

Just as sexual attraction and a desire to escape from a hampering set of inhibitions plays a part in the molding of Communists of both sexes, so a sexual attraction seems to help in breaking the bonds of the party. This can be true even when the upbringing was itself Communist. When Joseph G., whose story is told in Chapter Four, wrote out his account for us, his wife, Abigail, did the same. Here is her story:

"Almost as far back as I can remember, certainly by the age of 8 or 9 [she is now in her late twenties] my family had been in the Communist movement. My mother and father, both Jewish, emigrated from Russia and while never himself an actual member of the CP, my father influenced my two older sisters and older brother to join the Young Communist League in the thirties. I was at one time a 'Young Pioneer,' then a Y.C.L. member, and finally around 1940 a party member. I didn't much question the act of joining; it was almost my whole life, socially and otherwise, and the life of my entire immediate family.

"The family unit was a fairly happy one, in a medium-sized New England industrial town, and since I felt happy and content with my friends, my social life and in fact the whole environment, there never was a question of rebellion. I loved my father dearly and also one of my older sisters and my mother. Therefore, whatever those three said or did was gospel and right for me. They didn't question, so neither did I.

"My father was a worker in heavy industry and we were always quite poor, spending most of the thirties on relief, and so there were ample and obvious reasons surrounding our daily lives to make Communists of all of us. Those days, when I was between the ages of 9 and 16, I remember as vastly exciting the militant struggles constantly taking place against authorities in our city. My home was the center of all the activity, and I personally came in for a great deal of attention and admiration from the many leaders who visited and slept overnight at our house. Therefore, I assume, that when I became an adult and was ready to join the party, there were all of these nostalgic and very pleasant memories in the background. Besides,

I never felt any particular reason to refuse to follow along on the same path taken by the rest of the family. Such a step, I feel, would have led to my placing myself outside of this warm, human circle of family and friends of which I had been a part all of my life. Even had I the convictions to do other than join the party, I think now that it would have been impossible for me to make that break.

"Generally, as I have said, our family was in the lower income group. I was able to put myself through business school after completing high school and trained myself for rather highly paid and skilled work. This enabled me to move to a larger city, namely New York, where I continued my party activity but also where I met my future husband.

"He is writing his story also, so I need not go into it, but the fact that I did fall in love not only with somebody not in the party but an actual ex- and anti-Communist made me realize that I was slowly moving away from the party. Before I met him I had certain dissatisfactions with my detailed activity and various misgivings about the 'party line' but most of this I attributed to the fact that New York party members were different from those in my hometown, that it wasn't party policy I suspected so much as individual members and leaders.

"It took several years, in fact until after we were married, before I actually left the party, although I had ceased to be an active member long before. The big deterrent to my leaving was not my political convictions but my feeling that I would be betraying my family and hurting them irreparably. I feel that I was very fortunate in having my husband's help for otherwise, much as I may have wanted to leave, the nothingness to fall back on would have frightened me. And of course he opened my eyes and once I began to see the world as it really is, and not as it is to a Communist, it was impossible for me to remain a Communist despite my love for my family. Now I simply do not discuss any politics with the family; we avoid the issue, and since they do not live near me it is not difficult. If we were to discuss anything relative to the matter, of necessity bitterness and hard feelings would result, as they still are ardent 'believers.' Now I find it amazing, incredulous, and appalling that I could ever have been like them and terribly thankful that I am now a free human being.

"My experience, then, is that I got out once I broke away from my family and had elsewhere to go, so that I neither joined for an intellectual reason nor left for such a reason; the whole thing was always tied up with personal, social relationships. My belief in communism was 90 per cent emotional, 10 per cent intellectual.

"However, I do feel that I personally received certain benefits. I feel I will always be an aware, politically conscious person; that I came to love and appreciate fine things in art, music, literature through some of the relationships I'd made. It certainly, I feel, has made me a more responsible member of any community I live in. There is still that feeling that I should do something to aid human beings and humanity.

"My feelings now are that I personally should try to 'rescue' other Communists and help them to become free. A lifetime of Communist party training is difficult to shake off and I must still make a conscious effort to read things impartially, not as a Communist would. I think remaining members need outside help and encouragement. If published—and I hope they are—these stories should help considerably."

Greater awareness of the part that romance plays both in entering and leaving the Communist ranks is displayed by Florence W—. Born in the Middle West, she early set out to make a career which would take her away from home. At the same time, she likes to remember her childhood as happy, but there seem to be reservations.

She writes, for instance, that she had many childhood friends "although I didn't always make friends with those with whom I wished to." However, she realized her ambition and after a brief period as a magazine research worker, she applied for and obtained a post with one of the New Deal agencies.

The work was exciting to her. She had entered a world where for the first time she met a great many people who shared her interests— "Similarity of social philosophy has more often than not been a real factor in my adult friendships," she writes. In this frame of mind she met a man of whom she says:

"I thought I was in love with one lad who was involved in all these same activities. He had a greater dedication of purpose than many of the others."

He was also a Communist, and Florence married him the same year that she joined the party. She adds:

"My devoutness and sense of dedication to this cause continued to increase for about a year and a half. This period roughly coincides with that of my first marriage.

"I probably should not have left the party when I did had I not met a young man whom I liked immediately and shortly loved deeply. To him the party was not an anathema, but he found other methods of reform intellectually much more appealing and honest. I wanted desperately to be accepted by him and felt I could not be as long as I was a member of the party. It was with his full knowledge that I made my decision to resign.

"I had been thinking of leaving the party but lacked the necessary impetus. For one thing, there had been a stooge in the organization a few months earlier, and I didn't want my leaving to seem an act of cowardice. The local party organization had become weak, ineffective, and loosely organized, and with this deepening personal attachment to one not a member of the party I no longer felt the need to keep up my membership. On the contrary, I wanted to make a clean break with the organization. I tendered my verbal resignation to the local party organizer in mid-1939, three months before the Hitler-Stalin pact, and immediately felt a great sense of relief to have 'cut the cord.' "

Florence had obtained her divorce only a matter of weeks before her resignation, and married her new love later the same year. Under these romantic circumstances, she had fewer of the fears that afflict most departing members.

"I was not afraid of being blackmailed if I got out," she writes; "I was concerned that I might be condemned by my friends who were still members. I had no denials of membership to defend; I had made none."

As a happily married woman, Florence gave up work outside the home. She had received a plain intimation that promotion would never come her way since she admitted to having once been a Communist. She did not and does not want another job, so the main difficulty she has encountered has been her reluctance to testify as to who was a member in her time.

"It was not until about 1946 or 1947," she writes, "that I was willing to believe some of the statements about the Communist party that I read in the daily newspapers. My own experience had been so different and had in no way involved sabotage, subversion, or other illegal acts. Nor did I have any knowledge of their being committed by other party members. The Communist party, in the limited area in which I knew it, was closely identified with the labor movement and was a catalytic agent for heightened activity therein. I never considered it a foreign-dominated political movement as charged by the press."

The male counterpart of this typical feminine experience in the party is exemplified by Alexander Y—, whose childhood was a repetition of so many of the upper-educated, upper-income group. Alexander is a good deal more philosophical about communism than most of those who wrote for us. Perhaps because he has a good and responsible job in Europe for a big American firm, he has been able to take a more detached view of the party. As he himself says:

"Were I a citizen of England or France, I would not insist on writing this anonymously, for in those lands the social climate allows people to admit error, that is—admit a former membership in the Communist party."

Looking back at his rebellion against his parents—the conservatism of his father and the piety of his mother—and at his budding idealism in college, he nevertheless says:

"If any one person got me into the party it was a friend of my sister. I was in love with her at 20 when she was 18—and a sophisticated 18; 'wild,' my mother called her. She had joined a CP group at high school and remained with it at college. She told me she was fed up with words and felt the need for actively working for the betterment of mankind.

"Getting into the party is fairly simple. You sort of slide in if you need a group, a feeling of belonging to an organization. My college fraternity nearly supplied that need for me, but I wanted K. and K. was in the party, so I joined. Sister came along out of interest and curiosity."

Alexander and K. were married, and lived happily in the party for a time. They have two children now, and Alexander thinks his "work habits were improved by an activity in the party." He attributes some share of his substantial income to this fact.

"Getting out is much slower than getting in," he says. "It requires another kind of rebellion, a rebellion in which the center of the battle is yourself without any defined adversary. Normally the escape is carried on in two's, just as the entrance is seldom one by one."

In Alexander's case, he found K.'s desire to leave coinciding with his own, if indeed his was not influenced by her.

"I was ready to stand on my own feet, provided I held K.'s hand," was the way he put it.

In all these cases, and in a great many more, the departure from the party is made by couples even if one of them entered the party alone. It is also true of a great many former Communists who have written their experiences for publication under their own names, although as we have said we do not regard these as quite typical of the rank and file.

Hede Massing, wife of Gerhardt Eisler, says in *This Deception* that she made up her mind to get out of the party while "in bed" with her then husband, not a Communist. Charlotte Haldane, in *Truth Will Out,* got into the party while tending toward marriage with the scientist and Communist, J. B. S. Haldane, and got out while in the course of divorcing him. Elizabeth Bentley, who was a Communist courier, thought of leaving the party only after her lover, Jacob Golos, Communist leader, had died.

It is a fact, of course, that being able to go out with a partner or go out to a partner who understands, even if not a member, helps remove that dread of loneliness which is one of the obstacles to resignation.

In a good many instances there seems to be a certain undercurrent of sexual disturbance in the lives of those who are about to withdraw from the party. This often, as in the case of Edward C— and his wife, centers around some differences as to whether or not they should withdraw, with one partner more eager to do so than the other. Even more frequently, however, this disturbance appears in the lives of already disturbed people.

There is no way of knowing as yet whether Communists are any more prone than others to seek a sexual partner in the image of a parent—whether women fall in love with party members whose personalities resemble the girls' fathers and whether boys are seeking replicas of their mothers. They do not know this themselves, and even more than the average seem inclined to discount the influence of sex. This denial is quite natural, for it would be a great blow to self-esteem to admit even to themselves, perhaps especially to themselves, that adherence to a movement billing itself as the hope of mankind was related to a mere instinctive drive.

As has been evidenced in the accounts written for us, the tendency seems to be that in Communist marriages the wife is the more dominant partner. There is some evidence that this becomes progressively more true the higher up the hierarchical party ladder one climbs. Thus, it was generally assumed among Communists that Earl Browder was henpecked.

Sex, therefore, seems to play its part in the personality of the Communist as it does in the personality of anyone. While it is true that there is not a Communist under every bed, the Freudians would have a good deal of justification for the claim that there is a bed under the basic emotional motivations of every Communist.

〰〰〰〰〰〰〰〰〰〰〰〰〰

CHAPTER ELEVEN

COMMON GROUND

ONE feature of the usual American attitude toward communism—whether combating it, analyzing it, or sympathizing with it—has been a tendency to consider it in terms of ideology or philosophy rather than people. This leads to abstractions and misconceptions rather than facts. It is an error to which the Communists themselves are prone. They are concerned, they often say, with a cause rather than with the individual. This is for them a matter of principle. But for most of us the individual is important, and a cause is of value only as it affects people. In fact one basic, irreconcilable difference between Americanism and communism is our belief, which communism denies in action, that human beings are more important than human institutions. Therefore, it is a mistake to look upon communism as more important than Communists. It is a mistake, too, which contradicts one of the chief tenets of democracy.

The people who make up the Communist party in this country are special kinds of individuals. Not just one kind.

First of all, there is the gulf that separates rank-and-file membership from the leaders. The rank and file is a relatively numerous but shifting body which is constantly changing as the disillusioned or the disappointed or the indifferent drop out and new recruits join. The average length of general membership is between two and three years, probably nearer three. The hard core of the party's leadership is composed of men and women who, like the rank and file, generally have joined young but unlike the rank and file become fixed in the psychological pattern which led them to take up membership. They are able to accept completely the subservience toward Russian politics and Russian leaders. They are themselves much more likely to be foreign-born than is the rank-and-file member. It is also significant that in the very top echelon of this leadership there is not a single individual who has achieved any reputation for talents outside the party, although such individuals occupy many lesser posts.

It would appear to be true that, more than in most other organizations in the United States, there is a chasm between the rank and file and the leaders. More than in most other organizations, the leadership commands and the rank and file obeys. There is little effort by the leaders to persuade or cajole. There is no chance for the rank and file to ever suggest policies or choose between two leaders. When Browder became head of the party after a confused interval in which Foster was deposed, the order came from Moscow; the membership was not consulted. When Foster replaced Browder again, it was the same procedure. The membership is without affirmative or veto powers.

The leaders are content with this (except perhaps the ones who are deposed), although they know it is one of the features of their organization which keeps them a small minority group. They do not seek more. It is part of their belief that no matter what setbacks they suffer now, communism will triumph in the end. They do not think they can defeat the present American system by any recruiting or propaganda. They count upon us to defeat ourselves. They are quite sure that we will get both our economics and our politics into such a state of confusion that communism will take over as the only group with a program. Even in Russia, the party was never very numerous in proportion to the population; it took advantage of the downfall of a regime to assume power; once in power, it preferred to keep party membership for the "elite." Permanent minority status does not appeal so greatly to the rank and file; they look to a day when they will be numerous, and it is one of the causes of disillusionment when they find that this is not only unlikely but undesired.

In the first-person stories which have been quoted in previous chapters, and in the many more told to us which are so similar that they have not been quoted, certain patterns have been found. But in addition to these, already discussed under the various chapter headings, there are some other trends which seem to appear whether actually stated by the individuals or not.

Whatever the combination of psychological factors that led the individual into the party, almost invariably it seemed to that individual that his motives were entirely idealistic. In fact, almost to a man and a woman they began by pointing out that their motives were the betterment of society through fighting war or fascism or discrimination or poverty or some other form of underprivilege and injustice. Yet as the story unfolded, each became aware of circumstances in upbringing or emotional development which were even more compelling. They clung to their insistence upon the idealistic motive even as they explained that a reaction against parental influence or a desire to follow a lover or a sense of relief in finding an infallible absolute guide or a need to belong had been the powerful factor in Communist membership.

As far as they could see, they were right in so insisting. The factors that make up any personality are so entangled that the individual almost never can separate them completely in his own thinking. Besides, despite the profound importance of these other reasons, the fact remains that the rank-and-file Communists are idealists. They are selfless and dedicated people, even if they were made so by a craving for self-satisfaction. They cannot safely be dismissed as neurotics or posers or fakers. They are quite sincere when they tell us that in the Communist party they seemed to find the most dedicated, if not the wisest or most honest, fighters against fascism or the noisiest crusaders for racial equality or the most dramatic proponents of justice for sharecroppers or the unemployed. They sincerely confuse demagogic promises for paradise tomorrow with secret plans for totalitarian dictatorship.

The average Communist seems to be distinguished from non-Communist believers of the same ideals by an absence of individual grace and humor. Lacking in whimsy, in the magic of human relations, they go at even their recreations in a mood of anxious solemnity. They are people who, even when walking through a lovely countryside, are so absorbed in themselves and their cause that they never see the trees and streams and flowers. When they dance, they go in for group rather than partnership affairs, square dances which avoid intimacy. When they sing, they strike up the consciously stimulating aggressive music rather than the soothing or relaxing songs, and they avoid Negro spirituals out of a mistaken notion that these are a mark of racial discrimination.

They are verbose to an almost frightening degree, and yet in a way they strike one as being rather silent people. This paradox springs from their apparent belief that communication was given to man only for purposes of argument or exposition, never for a free exchange of ideas or even of nonsense. Their attitude toward time is as contradictory as their attitude toward talk. They are a little frightened of leisure; they want to be doing something, but anyone who has sat in at a meeting with them will have been sorely tried by their love of remaining endlessly at the conference table or the meeting hall. Of course this is a conscious tactic; Communists often have captured an organization by the simple process of outlasting their opponents, listening to their leaders repeating the same words over and over, and then voting when those with smaller capacity for sitting have gone home. They could not do it so well if it were not natural to them.

The average member enjoys subordination, seeming to derive an almost spiritual satisfaction by subjugating his will to that of superiors. This does not make him feel any the less important. On the contrary, it is likely to add to his sense of power, for he becomes a part of something much bigger and stronger than himself. In much the same way, the devout communicant of a religion is far from diminishing himself in his own eyes when he sinks himself in the body of the church. In this spirit, the Communist party can command many sacrifices—sacrifices of material advancement, of home and family. It is with a sense of exaltation that many members move, on party orders, to a strange community or change jobs or accept a personally distasteful assignment. This is one explanation of the readiness with which Communists consent to spy on one another, to betray confidences of those outside the party, even to become part of an espionage or sabotage ring.

Whether they like the secrecy and deception or not, most Communists recognize it as essential to the movement. As they grow accustomed to lying to their non-Communist friends, their family, their employers or associates, many of them develop a pride in their ability to deceive. This comes in large part from their realization that they are not doing it for money or personal advancement. There comes to some a sort of pleasure which is like that of the small boy playing at being a G-man. It is also what makes the Communist spy so difficult to detect, since for the first time in our history we have the phenomenon of our national betrayal by Americans not for money but out of conviction that another country is better.

The necessity for deception makes membership in the party a constant challenge. A certain kind of strength is needed for survival. The party has been compared to an overcrowded car to which passengers cling by bare handholds. The weaker ones are constantly falling off and being crushed. Some are thrown off as the car goes around curves; some just get tired of hanging on; some jump because they think they see a better car. And of course a few make their way safely inside among the leaders and stay there. The car, obviously uncomfortable as it is, keeps picking up new passengers because they think it is better than walking.

On the whole, the membership of the party seems to be likable if petulant. Meeting the average individual of the rank and file, we are impressed by the fact that here is a serious young person, eager to do good, a little too certain of all the answers but not very familiar with the questions.

There is a good deal of suspicion among them. It may be that their own motives unconsciously add to that quality. Their adherence to communism, ostensibly so idealistic and in reality so much a product of their own emotions, does not bear up under their own scrutiny while they are in the party. Why should they think that other comrades are any better? And if comrades can be suspect, everyone else can easily be looked upon as downright dangerous.

Mistrust of themselves and their immediate associates and everyone outside the party makes it all the more important for them to place implicit faith in someone or something. The bill is filled by the party as an abstraction, faraway Russia, and the remote figure of Stalin.

The inner insecurity of which suspicion is a symptom seems to stem from various causes, some relating to the personality of the individual and some to the circumstances of his environment. But whether they are caused by psychological factors or the pressure of family and society, they tend to make a philosophy of absolutes attractive.

Many Communists seem to us to be just the sort of people who turn for security to the absolutes of religion. In the past, virtually every one of them could find what he was looking for in a church. But today religion has lost that hold upon many. It is not without significance that communism has many features of an organized church. There is the same reliance upon dogma, upon the importance of faith, upon acceptance of revealed "truths" which cannot be proved by reason, upon a blind hatred of heresy and apostasy. The success of communism may be a measure of the failure of the churches; the failure of communism, which is more apparent, may by the same token be a measure of the strength of religion. It is no mere coincidence that a good many Communists turn from the rigidity of the party to the most rigid of religions or the most autocratic spouses or a job with rigid routine. In weighing the reasons why ex-Communists join the Catholic Church in rather surprising numbers, it must be remembered that the great majority remain as indifferent to religion as they were before.

Implicit in the stories and the actions of many Communists is a desire for punishment. They are the modern equivalents of the fanatics who used to mortify the flesh by rigorous penances. In this country at least, we find that Communists are more desirous of martyrdom for themselves than of terrorizing others. This tendency is encouraged by their leadership, for martyrdom pays better dividends in our society than terror, even if communism were strong enough to attempt the large-scale, spectacular inquisitions which seem to be a feature of its rule in other countries. They would like more martyrs here because they know that in a country with a free press there often is no better way to give publicity to a man's beliefs than to kill him.

Communists generally are well grounded in the historical precedents and philosophical arguments for Russia's current line. In part this is because they are a highly educated group. Few other public organizations contain so high a proportion of university graduates. They are usually fairly studious individuals, and the party's emphasis on education further indoctrinates them in the literature of which the leaders approve. An outsider usually is struck by the amount of time Communists must spend in reading and attending lectures.

The relatively smaller number of manual workers in the party is evidence of the bourgeois nature of the membership. It is, so to speak, a renegade bourgeoisie eager to escape from the hated class in an effort to escape from self. The relatively few workers in the party accept as a necessity the manual tasks of packaging literature, running mimeograph machines, carrying picket signs. The majority, the men and women who have always had white-collar jobs, rejoice in these tasks. They seem to be surprised not to meet more people who work with their hands and yet are not engineers or physicians or chemists. Their stories abound with such remarks as:

"I met no workers in the party. All the Communists I knew wore hats or no hats; none wore caps."

Or:

"The only fellow members who looked as if they knew how to handle tools were a few engineers and radio technicians."

The show of emotions is also a little different from what we might expect, considering the nature of the homes and schools from which most members of the party come. Of course a show of emotion is quite distinct from having the emotion. Most of the upper-educated, upper-income groups in this country display their feelings in public with considerable facility. This is or appears to be much less true of the Communist. They do little crying over themselves in public, although they may do much weeping for society. Yet from what we read between the lines of their stories rather than from anything actually said, we suspect that there may be a good deal of crying over themselves in secret and with a considerable sense of guilt for this weakness. This guilt arises from the very severe stunting of emotions which is part of Communist training. The individual is supposed to reserve his intimate feelings for the cause. He is supposed to subordinate his own personal emotions.

This discipline may stem from an apparent Communist belief in a sort of original sin. Communists seem to think that every human being is born with a bundle of antisocial attitudes within himself. Communism and work for the cause redeem him.

All this indicates that the average Communist is an extremely contradictory personality. His emotional conflicts seldom proceed to the point of mental illness, but they confuse him and those who would study him. The danger of resolving these conflicts is recognized by the higher powers of communism. The leaders have regarded psychiatry as a more basic enemy than the law or the FBI. They know they can lose most of their followers once these followers understand their own emotions. That is why the prohibition against consulting a psychiatrist or psychoanalyst, unless vouched for by the party as uninfected by Freud, is as firm as the prohibition against associating with a Trotskyite, although there is some evidence of an effort to work out a system of Marxist psychiatry.

Would the idealistic, rebellious children of well-to-do parents whose stories have been presented here have remained in the party as long as they did if they had understood their own motives? What would have been an analyst's interpretation of the account written by Elizabeth Bentley, former Communist courier, who wrote freely of her whole life but scarcely mentions her father, who says she joined the party as a cause of which her mother would have approved, and notes that the lips of her Communist lover reminded her of those of her mother? What happens to a boy who sleeps with a pen knife under his pillow, has a brother who commits suicide, a father who deserts the home, and an in-living grandmother who is crazy? Can he live without joining some dictatorial group that symbolizes warmth, even if his name be Chambers?

Of course there are contradictions in all of us, but the special contradictions which afflict the ex-Communists are sometimes revealing and sometimes pitiful. Sometimes, too, the individual seems to have left the party as a result of having got rid of his contradictions.

In the party, for example, rank-and-file members are extremely humble in their attitude toward party leaders. Yet they do not seem to have very much humility in their characters. Pride, a certain intellectual arrogance, appears to be much more prevalent. But after they leave the party, some of them acquire a genuine humility. They no longer know all the answers. They are willing to listen without scorn to points of view other than their own. We see this in the case of the young people who had been Communists at college, and were willing after they left the party to accept a majority vote in organizations they later joined even when the vote went against them.

Many if not most of the former Communists who have helped in this book suffered a genuine clash of loyalties when they came to leave the party. They wanted to get out and wanted it badly. They wanted to do it quietly and without fuss or they wanted to fight the party, but whichever way they felt, they were of two minds about friends who still were members. Unless the former Communist was quite without tenderness, he wanted to protect his friends or some of them, even when he wanted to give the FBI full information. He wanted it even more when he was reluctant to talk to the FBI at all. This was the case of a young housewife who suffered real anguish because she was asked to tell the names of individuals who had been party members in the thirties. It is the case even of those who have made the most public parade of their apostasy from communism and who have gone so far that they sometimes were accused of reaching out to implicate the innocent. This was true of Elizabeth Bentley who, in seeking out the FBI and in adding to her original story in a series of witness-stand appearances and writings, still kept wondering which old friends she could protect or tip off as to what she was going to say.

Certain experiences seem to be common to most former Communists, whatever their reasons for joining and leaving the party. This is seen more plainly among the anonymous rank-and-file members who gave us their stories than among those who have written for publication, since those who come before the public naturally wish to make their own cases appear to be unique.

As most former Communists look back on it from the more obscure position than a Bentley or a Chambers achieved, they feel that they were coming out from under an anesthetic. They come out into a period of painful self-examination, especially those who do not join other organizations immediately. They are unsure of themselves, and in the stories of nearly all we find them recalling a period of difficult readjustment to the new life, often lasting for years, as they acquire new habits of work and thought and, above all, of human relationships.

But most of them are lonely at first. They have left behind friends and the guides to whom they looked for leadership. They are doubtful of their reception in the world outside the party, and usually they are justified in their fears. They do not know where to look for new friends, and usually they are apprehensive about employment. There is no longer a set of infallible rules to live by, no easy road to appraisal of what is happening to themselves and the world. Old habits of suspicion and doubt are strong. Some of them seem to volunteer to give lectures to fill the gap in their lives rather than from any special desire to impart information.

There comes a time, however, when the former Communist feels relieved, released. He is able to enjoy a belly laugh again (someone ought to do a study of the differences between Communist humor and American humor) and to engage in idle conversation without watching every word that is spoken by himself and by others. He is able to hold his own opinions, even some of them Marxist opinions, without feeling that everyone who disagrees with him is a criminal or a dupe.

In the account of Lucille S— we find one of the most

representative stories of the mental and emotional development that takes an American into and out of the Communist party. She combines, as nearly all of them do, the many influences of education, family background, individual temperament. But she seems to be more aware of them than most. She writes:

"I am a woman who for over ten years was a member of the Communist party. From 1937 to 1948 betrayals, wars, purges, lies, manifest hypocrisy, and ideological about-faces left me untouched. What the party did, what Russia did, what happened in the world affected not at all my attachment to communism. During these years I worked at my career, married, and became the mother of two children. I saw my marriage fail and lived with my children apart from my husband. These experiences, just as events in the world, had little obvious effect on the core of my communism.

"Then late in 1948, a separated and nearly divorced woman, I went to a party at the house of a friend. I went alone. And I felt alone in a gathering of diverse people, mostly intellectuals and non-Communists—writers, artists, musicians, professionals. The types were familiar to me. But this party, unlike at least half that I had attended for 11 years, did not have the esprit which comes from everyone sharing common views. Being a shy person, reticent and inclined to sit silent, I was more at home, comfortable, and relaxed where I knew my opinions were not questioned.

"At this party people of diverse political opinions were not inhibited about voicing them. Instead of merging my dim personality into the group as a whole, I had to find an individual to whom I could attach myself for the evening if it was not to be an ordeal. I did, using one of those vague chances which every party provides. Before the evening was over I was in love. Just that sudden and swift. And I was, knowing it only afterward, headed straight out of the Communist party and into my second marriage. For the man I met that night was an implacable foe of communism. His intelligence, patience, and sophistication opened my mind as it had never been opened before. His love sustained me with the strength I needed to emancipate myself from the clichés and illusions I had carried, like crutches, for so long."

Lucille begins her story with the reasons why she left the party—the typical experience of the rank and file. But in those few paragraphs is some explanation of how she came to join, too. In them we see her need for dependence on some strong authority, her doubts of self, her inability to handle diverse opinions. Her background, in external details rather unusual for an American, provided just the sort of inner life which makes good recruiting for communism.

Born into a well-to-do family in the Northwest, she was the youngest of three daughters, and born late to her parents—both past 40 at the time. Before she was ready for kindergarten, the family moved to Europe where the father pursued rather abstruse scholarship. Lucille describes him as "in no sense a forceful person," frequently away from home on his studies, leaving the children to be raised by "Mother's 'progressive' theories." Lucille felt that her parents were "engrossed in each other, adopting an affectionate but rather detached attitude toward their three daughters." She writes:

"I was not taken too seriously by my older sisters or parents. I played up to this attitude of amused affection, but was lonely, felt misunderstood, and inwardly was not a very happy child. I bitterly resented my mother's saying that I was more like her grandchild than her daughter, and that she could be more friendly with me than with my sisters because I had fewer problems. I pretended pride in the accepted fact that my oldest sister was Father's favorite, the next Mother's, so that I came off best as both were fond of me without competition.

"All this made me constantly on the lookout for substitute love. I lavished it on an older student (never a contemporary), a teacher, or at a later date an unattainable man."

Lucille's education was entrusted to a governess when she was small, and then she attended a series of European boarding schools. She grew up relying upon her mother's judgment, looking to her as a "goddess." She disliked her father who could send her into a sick panic by questioning her about her school work and demanding quick answers to problems set her, "a panic when confronted with the need for expressing my opinions or my ignorance which has persisted throughout my life." Politics, world events were not discussed, at least in her presence.

"When I left boarding school at 17," she continues, "my parents unknown to me were separated. I spent a few months alone with my father. Presumably because of his own preoccupation with an affair he was conducting (also unknown to me), his only role to me was one of monitor. I, looking as usual for someone to love, mooned beneath the window of an American student and after much mooning began my first affair. Father asked no questions; I think he was embarrassed to talk to me about anything approaching the personal. He merely was harsh and disapproving. Mother was away, immersed in her own unhappiness."

In addition to the student, there was an older girl who greatly influenced Lucille at this time, a young woman of liberal if not radical tendencies who was passionately interested in the French Popular Front of 1936 and the defense of the Spanish Republic in the Civil War which broke out that summer.

"It was then that I consciously began to identify myself with the underdog, the oppressed," says Lucille.

She returned to the United States with her father, glad to do so since the student with whom she was in love was also returning. She enrolled at an Eastern college for women, not a happy venture.

"I was more mature intellectually than the rest but less so socially," she recalls. "College life seemed pointless, a country-club existence. I was nauseated by the girls' attitudes—'necking' in cars, espousal of Father's political credo, and so on. Most of them came from Republican homes. At a straw vote held before the Landon-Roosevelt election of 1936, Landon got all the votes but two—one lone Democrat and one Communist, mine. I tacked a scarlet copy of the Communist Manifesto to my wall. I had not read it, but the rebel gesture had to be made."

She left college at the end of the year, her engagement to the student being broken at the same time by the man, "who realized I was too immature for him." She came to the city, got a small job as reader for a publisher, and set up housekeeping on an allowance from her father.

"I hated to take it when I knew he disapproved of what I was doing, and I suppose took out my resentment in being even more what he would dislike," she says.

Lucille up to this point had never thought about being a Communist; that came "quite by chance." She had drifted from an affair with a married man, met while apartment hunting, into one with an artistic youth in a federal theater project, "an easygoing, ineffectual, not too serious Communist," as she describes him. Through him she met others.

"They saw me as possible recruit material," she writes. "But when I, eager for any new allegiance that would give me some sort of anchor and security within the framework of my idealistic concepts, wished to join right away, they held me back. At their suggestion I attended a waterfront unit meeting. I also had joined a union, the Book and Magazine Guild. I would have been shocked then if anyone had told me this local was undemocratic and Communist-controlled. But in truth it was. The majority of its officers were Communists. Those who were not were called 'red-baiters' if they took an anti-party-line position."

Actually it was another young woman, daughter of an associate of Lucille's father, who got her into the party. Lucille met her on one of her infrequent visits to her parents, who were formally living together again and disagreeing about everything.

The most important experiences of Lucille's party membership were a couple of affairs, the first with a boy met at a pier when she was seeing her parents off to Europe and he was seeing off a group of volunteers for the Lincoln Brigade.

"With this affair began my interest in Spain. When the job of chairman of the Spain Committee in the union fell vacant, I volunteered. As usual, my emotional enthusiasm was far greater than my ability or inner desire to perform. I got complete stage fright and only held the job for a few months. Work for Spain held my interest less than the personal relationships involved. I lost interest in the boy, who was being groomed for further party work at party schools, and formed a new tie, again with a veteran of the Spanish war. He also was married. He was older, bitter, wiser, but not actively an anti-Communist. Knowing my blind allegiance, he did not articulate his doubts. I lived with him, supported him in part, for about two years.

"During this time, in a moment of shame at my ineffectuality in the union unit, I joined a 'concentration' unit in the machine industry. My job was to hand out the *Daily Worker* at a plant entrance. It was winter. I developed pneumonia and was hospitalized."

For several years, Lucille suffered recurrent bouts of illness in the winter, and "did no further work for the Communist party. I attended but few meetings, and was in short a parlor red only. But the crutch remained and the knowledge of my party card sustained me." At this time, a girl she had known in Europe arrived in this country and the two took an apartment together.

"It was this girl who looked after me when I was in the hospital with pneumonia and during convalescence; it was she who gave me money for an abortion, who sympathized with my need for love and anchorage. She too had many affairs, far more than I. She was not a Communist, but intellectually she followed the line pretty much. She and her friends were genuinely fond of me, and gave me a much-needed sense of belonging and being valued. I could keep my party card (we never once discussed the party, belonging to it, working for it, or anything approaching it) and yet be divorced from the responsibilities it entailed because I got companionship elsewhere."

The need to belong, which had not been satisfied in her family, had drawn Lucille into the party and was making her a nonactive member while in it. After her health was restored, she "became aware of the futility of my affair with the Spanish veteran, forced to the obvious conclusion that he never would get a divorce nor make money as long as I provided enough for him to drink." She got a job in another city.

"Before leaving," she says, "motivated by my fear of doing anything open to criticism, and not so much by any ardor, I inquired at the unit as to a transfer, and was told that someone would get in touch with me. No one did for months. Then I was called to the phone and a strange woman asked if I had my half of a dollar bill. I did not, and didn't know what on earth she was talking about. It finally came to me that she was talking for the party, but it seemed so ridiculous that I should begin finding the other half of a torn dollar bill that I had difficulty taking it seriously. On the other hand, the secrecy, cloak-and-daggerness of it scared me a little. I was suspicious of the caller and immediately antagonistic. To get off the phone I made an appointment which I never kept. No further approach was made to me. I had no contact with any Communist during my time in this city."

She did, however, meet and marry a young man who "while liberal was definitely no Communist." She told him she was, and "though he didn't like it, expressed no request for me to quit; his liberalism understood a respect for a person's politics." The young couple soon returned to New York and in intervals of bearing her children, Lucille worked as a researcher for a magazine.

"I had gone to a party meeting," she adds, "set my affairs straight with them, rationalizing my derelictions. I still needed the crutch. Once my excuses were accepted, I relaxed and tried to forget the whole thing. During the five years I was living with my first husband, I went to three meetings only, did no work, and evaded questions put to me by members sent to inquire at my home. Toward the end of my marriage, I pleaded emotional and psychological difficulties, talked of visiting an analyst, and in general received sympathy and little criticism. No coercive methods of any kind were at any time used on me. I paid dues when someone came to get them, once or twice a year. My resignation was given on the phone on the occasion of one of these check-ups. It was accepted on the grounds that I wasn't doing anything anyway, and that was that. Not one word from any known party member since, nor have I ever seen one."

Even without any activity by the party, Lucille found some difficulties in the final break. She writes:

"Emotionally I made the switch easily; I was in love. But the habits of many years do not slough off with a shake of the shoulders and it was a painful business. I began to think, to analyze my intellectual and emotional processes, my approaches and attitudes toward people, situations, and problems. The fact that at this time I was undergoing psychoanalysis while in a sense making the going tougher because I couldn't honestly evade thinking, facilitated the change and the self-probing. I stopped seeing my old friends. Psychologically I could not stand being with those who disapproved of me."

At the same time she felt no bitterness toward the party, perhaps "because I had never been confronted with dictatorial methods, assignments contrary to my own ethical code, evidence of betrayals, callousness, and so on. If the units to which I belonged engaged in espionage or treasonable activities, I did not see it. But it may have been going on all the time, for my innocence of mind undoubtedly affected everything I saw."

"Looking back at this personal story, I wonder if it is a common one. It seems unbelievable that I should have remained so free, so unmolested in my personal and intellectual life. No demands were made on me that I could not avoid. The only possible answer seems to be that from the first this child of bourgeois intellectual background could never be regarded as anything more than deadweight, dilettante, and suspect. And they were right."

While undoubtedly more dilettante than most, or at

least more willing to admit it, Lucille's story is one that could have been written by almost any of the former Communists over the years, so far as it portrays emotional development. The characteristics common to party members are the same among the hundreds who contributed their stories to us whether membership was taken and dropped in the 1920's or last year. The accounts of membership during the height of Russia's war popularity are hardly distinguishable from those of membership during the years of our current struggle with Russia on the international front. Neither the wild vagaries of the party line nor the tremendous shifts in public opinion nor the world-shaking events of the last 30 years have affected very much the nature of the individuals who join the Communist party of the United States.

The one exception is a group who became Communists during the depths of the depression. Here alone we find men and women driven by a desire to change an economic system by which they themselves were handicapped.

~~~~~~~~~~~~~~~~~~~~~~~~~~~~~~

CHAPTER TWELVE

BENEFITS

AMONG the former Communists who have contributed their stories to this book, Dorothy I. seems to us notable because she approaches so nearly what most of us consider "average." At first glance her individuality escapes notice because she looks and acts and talks like a lot of other people, none of them outstanding enough in memory to be identified. Everybody thinks he has met her before, but can't quite say where.

Dorothy is nearly 40, medium in height and figure, unobtrusive in dress, voice, and manner. Her friends say of her kindly that she would be quite nice looking if she didn't have such heavy eyebrows. Actually the brows are the one feature that gives her face some distinction.

Her background is equally "average." She was born in the country, the second of three children, and was raised in Chicago where her father went into business after selling his family farm in Iowa. She went through school and college in about the middle of her classes. She was average in games, in dates, in reading, in fondness for the movies, in resentments against and affection for her family. If anything she was a little on the serious side, but not so much as to be noticeable or seem peculiar. That seriousness governed her choice of a career, social work.

Dorothy was about average as a Communist, too, with the exception that she remained one longer than most rank-and-file members. She had been out of college a year and was holding her first job when she married a young man who had been a year ahead of her at college and had become a member of the party. It was 1935 and Dorothy was 22 years old.

When she first told us about her reasons for joining the party herself, she explained that she wanted to help the underdog, to work for "social, economic, and spiritual reforms." She was strongly repelled by the Chicago political machine and could not reconcile the Democratic ward politics she saw in operation with the national Democratic administration. She condemned both because of the sins of the one nearest home.

But why did that make her a Communist rather than a Socialist, a Farmer-Laborite, or even a Republican? Dorothy, thinking back to her then state of mind, recalled that the middle-of-the-road attitude of her father, the complete lack of political interest displayed by her brother, and the contrast of their indifference with what she saw of political evils in her own city were powerful arguments for going to extremes.

"And of course I was in love," she added. "The views of my husband seemed entirely admirable and his arguments unanswerable. I was proud to join him in what I thought was a modern crusade for the brotherhood of man."

Once in the party, Dorothy's unobtrusive efficiency and docility won her the privilege of doing a great many party chores. She soon became an organizer and remained in that capacity for a little more than ten years. In all that time no member of her family, except of course her husband, knew that she held a Communist card. Many women stay in the party if they attach themselves to "leaders" but Dorothy's husband was not one of the big shots in the movement.

Her husband was as hard a worker as she, but she now thinks that the very intensity of their party enthusiasm tended to cool them matrimonially. At any rate, by the time of World War II, they were no more than friends, not even very close co-workers, for his job took him away from home a great deal, while she usually was at some sort of meeting on the evenings he was at home. They had dedicated all of their lives to the party and that left nothing over to care for and nourish the marriage. Before the war ended, each wished to end the marriage, Dorothy because she had met another man.

This was just at the peak of Russia's popularity in this country as a wartime ally. Yet Dorothy found herself slipping out of sympathy with communism, she who had retained all her enthusiasm through the purge of Old Bolsheviks, the Stalin-Hitler pact, the Finnish war. She told us that she thought the Soviet government was displaying imperialistic tendencies; then she smiled and said that this probably was a rationalization on her part designed to mask an emotional reason for ceasing to be a Communist.

"I was in love again," she explained, "and just as had been the case ten years before, I found the arguments of the loved one very convincing."

Her divorce was not difficult, since her first husband was almost as eager for it as she, and she remarried in 1947. At the same time she dropped out of all her former activities and quietly withdrew from the Communist party without explanation or argument. Employed as a social worker by one of the leading welfare agencies, she is now regarded highly in her profession. She has a happy home, which is reflected in the good humor and good sense she brings to her job. She believes that the experience of ten years in Communist work makes her a better-adjusted human being and a more efficient social worker.

"I do not think I would have developed as good work habits or the willingness to study if it had not been for the discipline of the party," she says. "Along with the habit of talk—not such a good one, I admit—there was a lot of hard work. I got used to the idea that there is value in the dull routine things that I would have tried to dodge, I am sure, in any other environment I was likely to find. It was the same with many others I knew in the party.

"Then for the first time I learned to study. It had been easy to get by in college without concentrating very much. It is true that the Communist 'curriculum' was very strictly limited to the commie line, but since I have left the party I find that I have developed a knack for getting quickly to the meat of a book or a lecture. I have learned to organize what I read or hear in my own mind.

"Some of my friends and some of the girls I work with are awfully proud that they never do anything menial, as they call it. That means they won't carry a lot of packages or pitch in and help stamp envelopes in an emergency or get their hands dirty running a mimeograph machine. Maybe that's as close as I came to being a member of the proletariat, but I'm not a bit ashamed to get a little dirt under my fingernails. It'll come out.

"On the whole, I think the people I work with and my family are better off because of what I learned as a Communist, to the extent that it made me a better worker. I think, too, that we helped some of the good causes that the party stood for. While the commies were interested in organizing labor so they could make use of the unions, the fact remains that they did help make some unions strong and did teach some valuable labor people how to organize. Some of our best democratic labor officials learned their jobs while members of the Communist party. We should remember this without forgetting how much it cost some of these same unions to get free of commie domination.

"For myself, I'm glad that I fought hard for a better break for the unemployed and for families on relief. I'm not ashamed of the talking I did on behalf of low-cost housing although Chicago is hardly anything to boast about in this respect. I am ashamed that I fought for these things from within the Communist party. I know now that they are more likely to be won by other methods than the commies used, because the commies don't really want these reforms. They want to use the lack of them to win their own game. But under the circumstances as I knew them from 1935 on, there was quite a lot of good to set off against the harm caused by commie activities in this country."

Like Dorothy, a great many former Communists think they and society benefited from their membership in the party. Those who were members only in their late adolescence and early maturity think the experience helped them grow up. Nearly all those with whom we spoke, whatever their age when members, speak of the discipline of work and study as helping them later. Most of them seem to us to have been well qualified by temperament for work and study; they would not have been idle drones, in our opinion, in any case. But they might not have acquired such good habits in this respect without the rigid discipline of the party.

We have found that this feature of Communist life made such a strong impression that some young people upon leaving the party are disappointed and disgusted with the lack of hard work in other organizations. They say that in the new groups they join—if they join any—there is a lot of talk but nobody does anything. They remember their days in the party as a constant succession of doing things. They are willing to admit now that the things were not worth while or were positively wrong, but at least there was a real activity. And they were often too busy to worry about their own personal miseries.

The activity, of course, is one of the attractions that communism holds for many of its members, especially the youth. The habit of work remains with the former member; employers seldom complain of the laziness or incompetence of the former Communist, only of his possible loyalty.

In small towns and rural communities, the "therapy" of doing things is far more usual, since the people through their various organizations do for themselves many of the things which in big cities the people pay to have done. In the small town there is a wide variety of activity from helping at a strawberry festival of the church or taking turns cooking hot lunches at the local school to fencing a recreation ground or planting an invalid neighbor's garden. It may be that there is some connection between this common rural activity and the absence of Communist groups in the country towns and villages. In the city the average volunteer for the good of the community seldom gets a chance to do anything of so satisfying a nature. Even the well-to-do women who offer their time to hospitals and welfare agencies usually are looked down upon by the professional staffs or are assigned to the job of raising money, which is more closely related to begging than to work. During the war Red Cross activities, Civil Defense work, airplane spotting, all gave to citizens this necessary participation in community life.

Among other Communists who really were workers, the

amount of erudition they acquired from party work is astounding. Some of these people even surprised the Un-American Activities Committee. In the testimony of Joseph Kornfeder, known as Joseph Zack in the Communist party, the committee was treated to a quite lengthy and learned lecture on Communist theory and organization. Kornfeder had been a member of the party from its earliest American beginnings and remained in it for 15 years. He worked for the Communist International in South America, spent nearly three years in Russia at the end of the twenties, and became a Communist writer and district committee member in Ohio. He was a garment worker, but after he left the party in 1934—disillusioned by his Russian experience, he said—he spent a year reading "the pros and cons to Marxism." He was turned by his studies as well as his experiences against the Soviet regime and the American party although he still called himself "an adherent of the Communist philosophy as a general philosophy." As a garment worker, he then set himself to organize in New York a group which held forums and discussions on communism, and he was a prolific writer about communism. It is hard to believe that he would have acquired quite so much knowledge or studied quite so much without the discipline of the party.

From the standpoint of practical rather than psychological benefits, Benjamin U. is a rather striking example. He joined the Communist ranks when he was 16, and he owes his education as a writer to the party although he left it when he was 21. His family was poor and without enough political or social philosophy to be then—the early 1920's—much concerned about his communism. The boy showed enough talent to be encouraged and helped in the party, and he was benefited, he says, "very much."

As a boy Ben had been studious, avoided athletics, and

was rather unhappy. Apparently he chafed against poverty and lack of opportunity. He is Jewish, "but not then much conscious of it," he says now. He worked hard in positions of some leadership among Communist youth for five years and then adhered to the dissidents during the great Communist party splits of 1928 to 1930 when Trotskyites, Lovestoneites, and the rest were being expelled.

"The break is always primarily a *crisis of faith*—both emotional and intellectual," he says. "Membership in the party helped me grow up, taught me the facts of social life, inoculated me against 'liberal' naïveté. I think my pretty thorough study of Marxism has had a permanent and on the whole valuable effect on me."

As a writer, too, Ben thinks he has gained from the experience. Certainly he is more successful in his career now than he was when he held membership, but of course a part of that is his additional experience and maturity.

Benjamin U. is representative of the sort of youngster communism seems to make a special effort to attract, youngsters who will benefit and grow through the hard work and study which the party prescribes. As a group which seeks to be an "elite," a body of leaders for the coming revolution, the party wants people of talent and ability. It is significant that so many of them are repelled by communism when their intelligence and maturity give them a better insight into the real nature and aims of the party in the United States.

While in the party, many members learn one of the meanings of the word "sacrifice," a lesson which they share with the rank and file of a great many idealistic organizations. They derive a considerable satisfaction from earning less money than they might in order to work for the party which in their opinion will save mankind. They discover the joy of giving up material and even spiritual good for the welfare of others. It is a lesson they seldom forget after they have left the party, although they see the good being done in a far different way than they did while they were Communists.

Perhaps former party members we interviewed represent those who have benefited most. They have passed through the fierce fires of growing up, which for them often consists of admitting to themselves that they had committed an error, not just a small blunder but a cardinal mistake. They feel they have rejoined society after a period of wandering in the wilderness. It is a sort of rebirth, but painful. For in emerging from the darkness of communism into the light of free society, they must cut the umbilical cord themselves. Only then do they achieve independent existence.

The benefit an individual derives from a term in the Communist party is matched to an extent by gains which the nation can win by making intelligent use of these people. Specifically, the former Communist can be a far greater factor in defeating the party's long-range campaign to seize power than we have allowed them to be yet. The information they possess is invaluable; the FBI has already obtained a good deal of it. More would be forthcoming if it could be given without loss of self-respect.

In any kind of warfare, men trained in the ways of the enemy can supply data which is of prime importance in mapping strategy. This is the role of the former Communist, not to guide the strategy itself. They would be unreliable, inefficient in this respect, because very few of them are temperamentally suited to the task, and the very motives which impelled them to leave the party often cloud the judgment they do have.

The valuable information, furthermore, is not the names of other Communists. It lies in their understanding of the ways in which the party and the units of the party work, the approach they make to their ultimate goals, the objects of their propaganda, and so on. For example, one of our collaborators in speaking of his experience within the party used the phrase: "the final struggle for the sidewalks."

"That is how Communists expect to win," he explained. "When they can get control of the sidewalks by putting out mobs too big or too tough for the police to handle, they can seize power. Only after they have the streets do they go for the radio stations and the water works."

This gives a new outlook on Communist-inspired riots. Another former Communist, agreeing with this, pointed out that the party recently was toying with the idea of climbing to power on the back of a third party.

"Such a third party, built up so as to capture the nation in the 1960's, would be recruited among dissatisfied Republicans and Democrats, mild Socialists, minority groups, economically burdened small businessmen," he added. "The unifying core of such a movement will consist of concealed Communists. The bulk of it would be sincere people knowing and caring nothing about communism."

The former Communist in providing this ammunition against the party will help us avoid the danger to ourselves of using force. Nothing pleases the leaders of communism more than to be singled out as the targets for arbitrary forceful measures. For, as Walter Lippmann has pointed out, they think democratic governments will be destroyed "because in using force against the Communists, they will be unable to stop with the Communists. They will become involved in using force first against the fellow travelers and then against the labor unions and the progressives."

CHAPTER THIRTEEN

PRISONERS

NOTHING about a former Communist's story of his life in the party seems so baffling to many who hear it as his difficulty in leaving. Why, it is natural to ask, if a member has decided he wants to quit, doesn't he just up and do it?

In nearly all the stories already presented and in nearly all the rest we have seen or heard, the difficulty of withdrawal is one of the features which the teller emphasizes. Almost always it has made a great impression upon him, even to the point where he doubts that he ever would be able to nerve himself to do it if the situation arose again. The reasons for that difficulty are not always seen in the same light by the people who have passed through the adventure of communism. But in each case it seems to be compounded of the personality of the Communist, the nature of the party, and the attitude of the rest of society.

Looked at from their point of view, the length of time which elapses between the desire to break with the party and the actual action is not so surprising. After all, a member of a church who has lost his faith in its teachings will be longer in making up his mind to leave it than he would take to resign from a club with which he is dissatisfied.

The Communist who has lost his faith in his party needs longer to get out than does a Republican or Democrat who takes issue with his, even a Republican in Maine or a Democrat in Mississippi.

Virtually every former Communist, including those who have been expelled, realizes the fact. Some say the party itself is to blame and some that the attitude of society is at fault. Very few think that there is anything in their own make-up that tends to keep them prisoners within the party long after they first think of getting out.

Among those who gave us their stories and remembered the details of their struggle to leave well enough to be fairly sure of the length of time involved, this period stretched over anything from a few months to five years. Only a few very young Communists put their disillusionment and their resignation together at the same moment with no breast-beatings of delay. As might be expected, the longer a member remained in the party, the more difficult it was to break. On the average, we would guess from our material that about one fourth of a Communist's membership in the party is spent in working up to the point of leaving it after he first began to think he should.

They spend this time in an unhappy state of personal disillusionment or disappointment but reluctant to take the position that the cause for which so much has been given can be a fraud. One who never has dedicated himself to something or someone he regards as infallible and eternal cannot experience the wrench given to his whole being by a reversal or a loss of faith. The Communist has abandoned independence in thinking. He has abdicated rule over his own mind. He needs an internal revolution before he can get it back. Those who never have been in this position, who never needed the revolution, must exert a strong effort of imagination to understand how difficult it is for a revolutionist to revolt against himself.

Added to the difficulty of shedding any strongly held beliefs is the Communist's reluctance to admit personal error. Such admissions may be part of the patter at meetings or in conversations with other members where personal mistakes can be cited to emphasize the party's infallibility. But confession is confined to abstract details, never to a blunder which is of real importance in one's own life.

As has been seen, the bulk of Communists voluntarily choose the party, coming to it from other than Communist or even radical backgrounds. Few were children brought up in the party who matured to accept it as a matter of course. Furthermore, the majority not only chose membership but chose it because they wished to emphasize their hostility to something very different—to a dominating or overpowering or tyrannical parent, to a rigidly held reactionary or conservative code, to a sense of loneliness or frustration or inability to shine in some other group.

Everyone, but especially people like this, shrinks from admitting to himself that he has made a bad choice in a matter of first importance. It is easier to repudiate a way of life or a symbol to which one was born. But to give up as a mistake a way of life or a symbol which one has adopted out of the needs of one's own personality is another matter. As has been seen in the chapter on "home-made" Communists, it is easier to reject a natural father or mother than to go back on the father, Stalin, chosen deliberately as a substitute.

Loneliness and the disapproval of the group in which one lives—experiences relished by no one and tragedies for many—are particularly difficult for Communists to face. It seems to us that one of the strong motives for joining the

Communist party is to escape these two evils. From the material we have been able to assemble, it is clear that lonely, unpopular young people are often drawn to the party by the companionship and group approval which go with membership. For a person who has known these very real human joys only through communism, withdrawal from the party may represent a sacrifice of overwhelming proportions. It is no surprise that such a person hesitates.

The Communist's more than average desire for the approval of other people in his group—he can be quite proud of the hostility among those outside the charmed circle to which he belongs—is seen in the writings of what might be called the professional ex-Communists. These are the people who justify themselves publicly and profitably but (to do them justice) apparently are more interested in the publicity than the profit. It is seen, too, in the attitude of many former Communists who have testified before Congressional committees. It is more than the natural attempt to explain past activities in the best possible light. So far as the need for group approval tends to keep them in the party despite doubts or loss of faith, they tend to be kept prisoners of communism because of this trait in their own characters.

For example, Howard Bridgman, a professor of economics in Massachusetts, testified in 1950 when he was 38 years old about membership in the Communist party for nearly three years, from 1936 to 1939.

"I did not pull out as a member," he explained, "because many of the members were my friends. If I had pulled out it would have, in a sense, ostracized me, and I just didn't want to break with my friends."

Similarly, Richard J. Collins testified in the spring of 1951 that there was a certain something he did not understand that balked efforts to get out of the party. Collins, a screen writer, had been a member of the party from 1939 to 1947 and estimated that he had spent nearly 5,000 hours at Communist meetings. Finally he became "profoundly disturbed by the events following the Duclos letter." This document, written on orders from Moscow by the French Communist, Jacques Duclos, exposed Earl Browder, head of the American Communist party, as a heretic. Browder was propounding an outmoded party line which held that Soviet communism and American capitalism could cooperate in the postwar world. Duclos told the Americans that cooperation was off and the class war on. Browder was promptly ousted as party chief. A good many people besides Collins were shocked. And Collins also was unhappy over the lack of freedom for a writer in the party. But he added:

"It is hard to get out, not because anybody tells you you can't but because you have associations of many years, and you have liberal questions that you believed in together, and probably still do, and you have many hours of energy and time invested, and it is only when issues are sharp that decisions are made."

If Communists are the kind of people who find it difficult to cut their emotional losses, neither the attitude of the party nor of American society makes it any easier for them. The more the individual is sincere in his rejection of communism, the more his hardships in withdrawing are increased by these attitudes.

We would expect the Communist party to resent withdrawals and to prevent them in every way possible, by argument or threat or reprisal. The attitude of the rest of our society is less reasonable if perhaps as understandable. Compounded of fear and intolerance, it is not an intelligent approach to the problem.

As for the party, it has definite techniques for making

life miserable for former members. The knowledge that this is so, as has been repeated in a great many of the stories already told in this book, holds many Communists long after they had wanted to quit. If the doubter has made the mistake of denying Communist membership, he is particularly vulnerable. The comrades can betray him to the probable loss of job and livelihood. Even if there is no such handle, the threat to employment is more than most people care to face. In addition there may be anonymous denunciations to family and friends, harassment of children, petty annoyances, and the steady barrage of denunciation as a traitor, a Fascist, and a stool pigeon.

Fear of violence is a factor in the hesitation of only a few who wish to leave the party. They know that murder or beatings are not Communist practices in this country, but they cannot be sure that there will be no sudden switch in the party line. Or a decision to make an exception in one case might be just their hard luck.

The contempt which ex-Communists display toward anyone who leaves the party at a later date than they did hardly encourages withdrawal. The natural association for a former member would be those who go out. But unless he gets out with a group, he will have no one to talk to who has been through the same experience. He will have no welcome among the disillusioned of previous years. And he himself will not welcome those who get out later.

"It was different when I was in the party," is one of the most common sentences in the talk of former Communists of all years, and another is: "There's something suspicious about anyone who could accept the party line after that."

"That" refers to the event which the individual thinks finally caused his own disillusionment, whether it was the expulsion of Trotsky or the attack in Korea.

When the earlier convert from communism is in a position to use his prejudice against the later ones, as is the case we are told with some of those former members who are on the staffs of Congressional committees, his influence is correspondingly greater. His attitude may be punitive beyond the point where it is effective. Complete ostracism is something the most sincerely repentant ex-Communist may well fear more than any other punishment. Yet it is not at all an unreasonable fear, in the present state of mind which most ex-Communists themselves betray.

Finally, the disillusioned Communist's fear of the attitude of the rest of society usually is fully justified. The average non-Communist is more than a little dubious about accepting anyone who ever bore the party label. This point will be elaborated in the next chapter, but here we merely wish to point out that the general attitude which brands communism as the one sin which never can be expiated or forgiven tends to keep many members in the party.

The party's own record of cynicism and betrayal, the fanatic Communist's frequently open avowal of deceit as a tool which can be used without shame by his side are partly responsible for this attitude. But it may be unwise. If there is no hope of a job or a place in the non-Communist world, how can a Communist afford to leave the party? He may be certain in his own mind that he has no more sympathy with communism. He may be prepared to make a full disclosure of all that he knows to the FBI. But he may also feel himself trapped by an inability to support himself and his family economically and emotionally outside the fold.

This fear is strengthened when he sees non-Communists hounded because of a suspicion that they sympathized with or helped the movement. The party card-holder can and often does believe that if liberals who are smeared for mere association with a Communist or a Communist group can be ruined, the former party member will be in a hopeless situation. So the average rank-and-filer usually remains in the party for a good deal longer than he would like to, and a good deal longer than is good for society.

Of course the difficulties in withdrawal can be overemphasized. Obviously the rank-and-file member almost always does leave the party eventually in spite of fears and hesitation. The fact that there are about seven times as many of him as there were holding cards at the peak of membership is proof of this. They do finally manage to overcome the difficulties presented by their own personalities, by the party itself, and by Americans outside the party. Membership is a life sentence for only a few, and most of these become more important in the hierarchy than rank and file.

Nevertheless, it would be a gain for all of us if their term in the party could be shortened. Since they spend about one fourth of their period of party membership as prisoners of communism looking for a way out, this could be accomplished if we could create safely a climate in which it would be as painless to give up the party card as it is to drop a magazine subscription. By "safely" we mean without danger to the security of the nation. At present, disillusionment is not enough to cause an immediate break. An escape needs to be arranged. It still remains to be proved that our society is sufficiently interested in these prisoners to help them get away, and, collaterally, to deter others from joining.

CHAPTER FOURTEEN

A NEW PROGRAM
TO DEFEAT THE COMMUNIST PARTY IN THE U.S.A.

IF ANY one generalization emerges clearly from the study of men and women who have joined the Communist party in the United States during the last 30 years it is the fact that despite the twistings and turnings of the party line, communism always has appealed to the same kind of people. The recruits of the 1950's in temperament and background are very much like the recruits of the 1920's.

A national program for combating communism, therefore, should have as one of its main features a plan for speeding the sincere voluntary withdrawal of members and for disillusioning the susceptible *before* they enter the party rather than afterward. Since, over the years, there have been about 20 people who got out of the party for every one who is a member today, this should not be impossible.

If we want to do more than wait for the party in this country to destroy itself, we will have to take positive action to deprive it of members. Should that action be force or persuasion, ridicule or bribery? Should we proceed openly or by boring from within? Should we adopt measures to outlaw the party or remove the objects on which the party feeds? Should we buy members out, scare them out, drive them out, or lure them out? Is our best weapon jail or public opinion, suppression or free debate?

The entrenched leaders, the die-hard fanatics, the irreparably committed, are hard to move—as are also the very old people. But the accounts of former Communists, backed by the fact that for 30 years the Communist party has had an annual turnover of about one half to one third of its total membership, proves that rank-and-file joiners are susceptible to being drawn out of the party. If they leave in such numbers when it is difficult to do so, we are convinced that a rounded campaign of understanding and help would reduce the party within a year to the hard core. We are especially confident that almost all rank-and-file members under 30 could be drawn away from communism.

Such a program should be based upon these principles:

1. That the nation's steady progress toward economic and social justice should not be checked by hysterical outcries that Communists support or pretend to support measures which speed that progress.

2. That we reject the Communist self-appraisal of their own movement as based on economic truths; at the same time we recognize that membership in this country is not comparable to that in some other countries where it is based on hunger and despair, and therefore promise of mere subsistence or an acre of land has no appeal. In our land the movement is not a belly movement.

3. That since American Communists are motivated largely by psychological factors, these same factors must be used decisively in combating them.

4. That the bulwarks of American freedom, which are far more important than any other ideology to the welfare

of the people, should not be sacrificed through the frantic expedient of burning the house down to get rid of the rats, if for no better reason than that we know rats live in ruins even more happily than in the house.

No single measure can achieve the purpose. A concerted effort by many groups and all individuals is needed. The following program is proposed as an outline of procedure for Congress, other agencies of government, private and semipublic groups, churches, and individuals.

Action by Congress

The simplest action to indicate that our national legislators are gaining some understanding of the problem of communism in America would be repeal of the McCarran Act, and especially that section which aims at public registration of all members of Communist organizations or fellow-traveler organizations. This was a demand upon these people to step up and proclaim themselves pariahs and traitors. Human beings simply will not do such a thing. As might have been expected, the time limit for registration passed without any registrants.

The whole legislative trend against communism has been to seek to outlaw the party and therefore to drive it underground. By the very nature of the movement, a great deal of its activity is underground anyway; like an iceberg, only a small part shows. But it is folly to drive underground the small part that does show and so lose all the benefit of the warning. This also is the advice of J. Edgar Hoover of the FBI, whose experience and wisdom in this were overlooked by most liberals.

Furthermore, all human history proves the impracticability of outlawing an idea. We might be able to force the Communist party to change its name. In fact that has happened in the past. But it is neither more nor less of a menace under another name. The effectiveness of any law which outrages common sense is nil. How many Americans who liked a drink refrained from taking one from 1920 to 1935? How many motorists never exceeded a 15-mile speed limit? How many men and women who wanted to take a little flutter on a horse race or a numbers game refrained from doing so because it was against the law?

Instead of laws leading to more secrecy, we suggest laws that lead to more light of day. Except for overt acts of the nature of treason and sabotage—for which we have ample protection in law—the real danger of any organization seeking to overthrow American institutions stems from stealth. This is true of many more groups than the Communists. When they speak in their own names with their own voices they can be answered, and the public judges the worth of their ideas and their proposals. No subversive movement has made much headway through open advocacy. But when such groups pretend to speak in other names, when their propaganda is supposed to come from other sources, when their real support is mysterious or concealed, the people have no fair way of judging the merit of the idea. The right of everyone in this country to propound his ideas, Communist or Fascist or democratic, wild or sane, should be safeguarded. But the right of the rest of the people to know the source of the idea and the backing of the propounder is equally important.

Our freedoms are based on the principle that in the marketplace of thought, truth and justice win out. But that holds true only if there is free trade in the market. We think the rules of free trade should carry protection for society by accurate labels on the package. And we mean for all ideas that enter the market, particularly through our vast new techniques of mass distribution.

This can be achieved through reasonable disclosure of

the support and financial backing of each and every group or individual who seeks to influence the public through any form of mass appeal. No national lobby to the public mind can be conducted without the use of the mailbags. Without any trace of censorship of any material placed in the mails, Congress has the undisputed power to call for disclosure of the funds and people back of the printed material.

The President's Committee on Civil Rights under the chairmanship of Charles E. Wilson unanimously urged such procedure. Its report said:

"One of the things which totalitarians of both left and right have in common is a reluctance to come before the people honestly and say who they are, what they work for, and who supports them. Those persons in our own country who try to stir up religious and racial hatreds are no exception. They understand that the vicious doctrines which they advocate have been morally outlawed in America for more than a century and a half. This Committee is as eager to guarantee their civil rights as those of the people they attack. But we do not believe in a definition of civil rights which includes freedom to avoid all responsibility for one's opinions. This would be an unwise and disastrous weakening of the democratic process. If these people wish to influence the public in our national forum of opinion they should be free to do so, regardless of how distasteful their views are to us. But the public must be able to evaluate these views. . . . As recently as 1940, a study by the staff of the Senate Committee on Campaign Expenditures revealed that one third of the election propaganda in the campaign of that year was completely anonymous and that one half was partially and inadequately identified as to source and sponsorship. Moreover, the Committee reported that the anonymous material included 'the most virulent, dishonest, and defamatory propaganda.' Congress has already taken the first step to remedy this inadequacy by amending the election laws to forbid the distribution of anonymous campaign literature.

"The principle of disclosure is, we believe, the appropriate way to deal with those who would subvert our democracy by revolution or by encouraging disunity and destroying the civil rights of some groups. We have considered and rejected proposals which have been made to us for censoring or prohibiting material which defames religious or racial minority groups. Our purpose is not to constrict anyone's freedom to speak; it is rather to enable the people better to judge the true motives of those who try to sway them.

"Congress has already made use of the principle of disclosure in both the economic and political spheres. The Securities and Exchange Commission, the Federal Trade Commission, and the Pure Food and Drug Administration make available to the public information about sponsors of economic wares. . . . Thousands of statements disclosing the ownership and control of newspapers using the second-class mailing privilege are filed annually with the Post Office Department. Hundreds of statements disclosing the ownership and control of radio stations are filed with the Federal Communications Commission. Hundreds of lobbyists are now required to disclose their efforts to influence Congress under the Congressional Reorganization Act. In 1938, Congress found it necessary to pass the Foreign Agents Registration Act which forced certain citizens and aliens alike to register with the Department of Justice the facts about their sponsorship and activities. The effectiveness of these efforts has varied. We believe, however, that they have been sufficiently successful to warrant their further extension to all of those who attempt to influence public opinion."

We would like to see Congress take up this excellent statement, debate it fully, and pass legislation putting it into effect. Over the past decades, legislation in this direction has been introduced in Congress only to be diverted by attempts to limit disclosure to those organizations unpopular at the particular moment. We would oppose any type of such disclosure if imposed only on certain categories of ideas. No lobbying to the mass mind of our people should be anonymous or conducted under false titles and names.

Besides contributing greatly to free trade in the marketplace of thought, such a measure would greatly diminish the "clear and present danger" of Communist efforts in this country. It was Justice Holmes who enunciated the principle of "clear and present danger" as warranting actions which would be unconstitutional in the absence of such peril. Justice Brandeis added an important interpretation by which it is possible to define the term when it is applied to limitations on the freedom of speech and assembly. In effect, he said that if there was time and opportunity to answer the dangerous idea or to call the police, there was no justification for abridging the free expression of that idea. Full disclosure adds to the opportunity.

Furthermore, it is high time that our courts distinguished between secret and public speech and conspiracies. In the case of secret speech there can never be time to give answer or call the police, whether the speech is directed toward subversion of a bank, the city water works, radio station, or our nation.

Still another positive step would be the creation of a nonpartisan commission to spend a year in studying how to prevent subversion without destroying freedom. President Truman attempted to establish such a commission under the chairmanship of Admiral Chester W. Nimitz in 1951. The purpose was to conduct "a thorough study of the problem of providing for the internal security of the United States and at the same time protecting the rights and freedoms of individuals." Congress blocked the presidential effort, but surely such a commission is much needed.

Such a commission would not be suspected of perverting its function in favor of a pursuit of sensational headlines, a suspicion which dogs the work of the present House and Senate investigating committees. The commission would pitch its inquiry on a higher level than mere name-calling, which has been an unsavory feature of Congressional groups because of the activities of a few members of both Houses.

Establishment of such a commission would eliminate the need for public hearings by Congressional committees when those hearings involve individuals whether in the party or recently out of it. At present, the publicity of these hearings—whether it smears someone who never was a Communist, compromises someone who was once a Communist, or even exposes a current Communist—really achieves only two ends. The first is to keep in the party an unknown number of Communists, mostly young, who would get out if they were not afraid of being caught between reprisals by the party and ostracism by society. The second is to gratify the emotional cravings of those whose own inner insecurity drives them to seek the punishment of others.

The Congressional inquiries often have been called "witch hunts." While it would be dangerous to carry the parallel between these investigations and the Salem witchcraft trials to extremes, there is a useful analogy. The Salem trials developed as little truth about witches as the

Congressional investigations have about Communists. The hysterical courts of Salem seemed to desire only a confession, and immunity was promised to those who confessed. All of the accused preferred to burn. The Congressional committees also have been mainly concerned with confessions. They have obtained some, but the chief result has been that whether or not there was any implication of immunity, the witness burned anyway at the bar of public opinion. In Salem no one stopped to ask how these people were drawn into witchcraft, any more than Congress has tried to learn how Communists are drawn into the party.

It should be remembered that most of the factional information disclosed by the witnesses already has been supplied to the FBI. The value of such information to the public would be preserved by disclosure of the facts without the appearance of the individual at a public hearing. Of course witnesses in court proceedings are in a different category. Courts cannot operate in executive session in a democracy; a committee of Congress not only can but should in these cases.

If hearings are to continue, the committee staffs should be broadened and committee aims revised so that we may have some understanding of the real reasons why Americans join and leave the Communist party. The addition of a few clergymen, psychiatrists, psychologists, sociologists, and teachers to the committee staff would provide the expert advice and knowledge needed to get the material and evaluate it. A study of family backgrounds and experiences, of emotional development and the causes of the drift which led an individual into the party would be possible. The committees could do a definitive job along the lines which the previous chapters of this book have indicated. A week of such testimony would do more to inform the public and to destroy the party than years of hearings carried on in an atmosphere of bitterness and recrimination. An investigation along these lines could lead to a constructive program for preventing new membership and siphoning the present membership, save for the hard core of fanatics and saboteurs, out of the party.

Role of Goverment Agencies

Most Americans agree that the record of the Communist party calls for a considerable amount of police work if we are to be protected from Communist conspiracies. All of such police work should be left entirely in the hands of the government agency best equipped to carry it out, the FBI. Local police and even private groups should at most do no more than inform the FBI.

The concern of other government agencies is with what is called the loyalty program. The fundamental mistake in the program so far has been the failure to distinguish between sensitive and nonsensitive jobs in the civil service. Nine out of ten have no relation to security at all; it is a waste of time and a dangerous discrimination to try to keep anyone who ever was a Communist or a fellow traveler out of the nine.

Sensitive jobs may be of high or low rank. The sole question should be whether the post, because of the nature of the work or availability of information, is such that doubt of loyalty may not be tolerated. Of course proven disloyalty should be grounds for dismissal from any job.

For example, the man who empties the trash baskets in the White House might be able to get at valuable information, which should never be hazarded. Unless a former Communist had proved positively that he was trustworthy, he should not be employed here. But there could be no danger to the nation if he had a job emptying the trash baskets in the park. Even if such an employee were a member of the party, neither the state nor the people are endangered by his employment. This is especially true if his former membership was known to his superiors.

Groups Outside Government

The distinction between sensitive and nonsensitive jobs should be carried over into industry, private or semi-public organizations, and the professions. In defense plants, especially if it is feared there has been Communist infiltration of the union in the plant, this may present more difficulty than in government. But application of the principle would help make for protection. If labor were sure that only the genuinely sensitive jobs were involved and that the test was loyalty and not union activity, it would be easier to police the defense plants adequately in this respect.

While industries where the distinction is important have been working out their problems with little fanfare, the entertainment world has experienced the folly of blanket discrimination complicated by hysterical disregard for any such thing as evidence or even reason. People are condemned without hearings and in the absence of due process. To bar an actress or a dancer or a singer from appearance before the public because of suspicions—or even because of actual membership in the Communist party— is to take a stand with the bigots who would bar *Oliver Twist* from the movies, or keep Jews out of college, or force Negroes to sit in the back of the bus. The excuse, sometimes heard, that the employer does not believe the charges or does not think them serious himself but is afraid to be "controversial" is an aggravation of the offense. Americans who are so afraid of justice that they will not run a little risk for it usually find that they have made a bad bargain even in the profit-and-loss account.

The country's record on job discrimination, or perhaps we should say failure to apply proper job discrimination, against former Communists is a sorry one. The one consistently bright spot which we could find is provided by the Roman Catholic Church. Side by side with its strong opposition to communism, the church not only has successfully persuaded a great many Communists to leave the party but has undertaken to help them make new, respectable places for themselves.

This, of course, is in line with the Catholic doctrine that there is no sin so great that redemption after repentance is impossible. Furthermore, the Catholic Church is opposed to communism as such and is not swayed by fear of losing business or being thought red or being criticized —motives which seem to be as strong in some of the most vocal anti-Communists as any real hatred of communism.

Where such people spurn the former party member without trying to establish his sincerity or lack of it, the Catholic Church welcomes the former Communist, helps him overcome the loneliness which is the almost inevitable aftermath of escape from the party, steers him into a job if he needs one. If he fears reprisals from party members, the church will even find him a job in another city and help him move there so that he can re-establish himself in an environment where his past is not likely to catch up with him publicly.

Some labor unions, although by no means all, have displayed the same intelligence in their handling of the ex-Communist. A fairly large segment of the trade-union movement realized long before the rest of the country both that communism was a menace and that it only intensified that menace to drive the disillusioned party member to despair. Union leaders who had long, bitter struggles with Communists became aware of the large and rapid turnover in party membership. Some of them adopted the principle that the party would be weakened and the rest of society strengthened if those who wanted to get out were helped into jobs where their previous records were known, at least to the employer and the union officials, and not used against them.

The International Ladies Garment Workers Union, for example, fought one of the bitterest of labor struggles to drive Communists from positions of leadership. A Communist-inspired strike, called for the benefit of the party rather than the workers, almost wrecked the union. But the anti-Communist officials realized that they could not afford revenge even if they had wanted it. If they had declared war on every Communist to the death, no garment worker would have dared to have left the party. It would have been his only protection. But the ILGWU not only welcomed garment workers who left the party; it found jobs for men and women ex-Communists who had never worked in the industry. It is not irrelevant to note that this union is the particular *bête noir* of the Communist party.

In all this there is an obvious lesson for all civic, religious, and economic groups. The various churches, the Rotary and similar clubs, the American Legion and Veterans of Foreign Wars, organizations of business and of workers can take a constructive part in combating communism by helping deprive the party of its members.

The most effective would be a combination of employers and unions. We would like to see the National Association of Manufacturers, the Chamber of Commerce, the CIO, the AF of L, and the Railroad Brotherhoods join forces to establish an agency in every large city to find jobs for ex-Communists. We doubt that any one part of our proposed program would be so immediately successful in sucking out members of the Communist party. For, while communism in this country has a psychological rather than an economic base, Communists like the rest of us have economic lives. One of the greatest fears of the disillusioned party member is that he will lose his job and never get another. If he saw employers and fellow workers united to remove that fear, he would not spend one fourth of his time in the party nerving himself to get out. He could do it when he realized his error. Others might be prevented from joining if a societal attitude were so changed.

A great many organizations are in an admirable position to oppose communism through effective education. Others are able to contribute knowledge that would be invaluable. In the first group are such influential bodies as the American Legion. When these veterans promote a genuine educational campaign, they are doing a job that will harm communism at every point. But when they set themselves up as the judges of opinion, finding people guilty by association or even branding them as reds because of liberal views, they not only are committing gross injustice but are playing into the hands of the Communist party.

It seems plain in the autobiographical data we have presented from many of our collaborators that one reason they joined the party was a belief that it stood for economic progress and social justice. That belief is fostered far more by the outcry of those who think all such progress is red than by any claims the Communists can make themselves. An American Legion attack on Sarah Lawrence College is as good a recruiting campaign for communism as a smear by Senator McCarthy. Both are far more effective than anything the Communists can do themselves.

The second group of organizations that could perform a valuable service is made up of the professional associations of psychiatrists, counselors, clergymen, physicians, teachers, and sociologists. From them could come essential studies to provide the data on which we could base a more comprehensive program than is here suggested for preventing upper-educated, upper-income Americans from being fooled by communism.

The psychiatrists and psychologists could make an especially important contribution now. Since the emotional basis for the turn toward communism is certainly important and we believe predominant, the specialists in emotional problems could provide essential information. Their professional associations might address themselves to the task of collecting information from their members who have had former Communists as patients. (Few as yet have had actual Communists, since the party has determinedly discouraged recourse to this profession.) Such information, carefully edited to protect the anonymity of the patients, could be issued as a report on the real nature of the Communist. It should be an important guide to parents and teachers in the rearing of a generation that might escape entirely the emotional taint of communism. Analogous studies have been of aid in coming to grips with the bewildering personality of the religious or racial bigot.

Such a report might also be valuable in meeting what is bound to be another new twist in the party line, probably before the end of 1953. This will be an attempt to synthesize the teachings of Marx and Freud. In the past, Communists have written of the father of psychoanalysis as if he were a major conspirator against the safety of the Soviet Union. It was almost as reprehensible for a Communist to consult a psychiatrist as to talk to a Trotskyite. Actually the party had good reason to attempt to keep its followers away from psychoanalysis. In the Communist philosophy the individual must be completely subordinated to society. But the very nature of psychoanalysis exalts the individual. It is the exploration of the mind of one person with the help of one other person. Such individualism is anathema to a leadership which can hold its followers only through collective thinking. That is even more important a tenet of their so-called faith than collective farms or collective labor.

In the United States, however, it is not possible to keep such a highly educated, highly emotional group as the members of the Communist party from looking at the forbidden pastures. Some even stray into those pastures. The leadership's fear of wholesale defections from Marx to Freud is prompting a reappraisal of the psychoanalytic method. The next step will be an announcement that Freud was preceded in all essential points by a Russian scientist, and then there will be an approved Communist psychiatry.

Probably because of the emotional factor in communism, it sometimes has been suggested half jestingly that it might be well to organize a "Communists Anonymous" along the lines of Alcoholics Anonymous by which reformed party members could help each other toward rehabilitation. Actually there is enough anonymity in communism now. No more is needed.

There is a serious point behind the jest. The assumption of those who propose an organization of this kind is that the Communist is a sick person. We do not think that is true. He is not compulsive like the alcoholic or the drug addict; he certainly is not generally psychotic. Deviation from the approved conduct, such as joining the Communist party, is unreasoning but it is not a disease.

Schools and colleges have a role to play in the struggle against communism more important than harassing teachers suspected of nonconformity or liberal ideas, more important than weeding out possible pro-Communist statements from books in the library, more important even than finding and exposing a Communist on the faculty. Loyalty oaths are not objectionable in themselves but as a technique of locating Communists are absurd, since the Communists avow publicly that an oath is a form of bourgeois irrelevancy. The important role of education is to teach. Curiously enough, it has seldom been mentioned by the self-appointed reformers of the school system.

Surely the current struggle for the minds of men is serious enough to warrant consideration in the curriculum of the schools. We would like to see them introduce courses on underground movements in general. Students should have an opportunity to learn the truth about communism and the Ku Klux Klan. They would be better prepared to avoid membership in such organizations if they have assimilated some facts. We have faith in truth winning out and we have faith in Americans young and old—if given access to all facts and points of view.

It used to be thought that if children learned the truth about sex, they would promptly become promiscuous. Today there are people, some of them very influential with school boards, who think that if children learn the facts about communism they will promptly join the Communist party. They betray a sad lack of confidence in their own beliefs and their own institutions. A straightforward course without preaching or interjections of horror would strengthen, not weaken, attachment to the best principles of American life. Schools could be confident enough of our superiority in fact even to invite an avowed Communist to lecture in the course, where such a talk would be appropriate. That is applying the doctrine of free trade in ideas. For ideas are not like money. It is true that in a free market bad money will drive out good. But it is also true that in a free market good ideas will conquer the bad.

Coupled with these measures, and as part of the program for assuring free trade in the marketplace of ideas, non-Communist organizations of all kinds should be alert to point out objectively the fallacies in Communist reasoning and the deception which the Communists themselves practice. Name-calling is neither helpful nor convincing in this competition for the minds of men. Factual statements backed by evidence do the job better. One of the most successful of chain newspaper publishers once told a meeting of his editors that they should give up name-calling altogether. If proof is not offered that a man is well described by a dirty name, he reasoned, it does no good to call him one. If proof is offered, then there is no need to use the dirty name.

The Individual vs. Communism

Nothing distinguishes our society from that of Soviet Russia so much as our reliance upon the good sense and good faith of the individual. In the struggle against communism that reliance has been thoroughly justified. The public has generally rejected the hysterical extremists of both right and left. But it becomes increasingly difficult to preserve a balance. Each of us can help the others by acting on these basic American principles:

1. Keeping informed about the organizations to which we belong. It is not too much to insist that officials of all groups tell members what they are backing, who supports the organization financially as well as morally, just what activities are being undertaken. The member, in turn, should demand to know these things.

2. Disavowing all vigilante groups, no matter how powerful in the community. Vigilantes are those who take the law into their own hands. They are the ones who compile lists of people they call objectionable, set themselves

up as the judges of schools or speakers or books or radio programs, and organize boycotts usually with secret funds. The FBI can get along well without this competition and resulting confusion.

3. Demanding overwhelming evidence after proper hearings before branding an organization or an industry or an individual as Communist. (Or Fascist or anything else, for that matter.) It has become common talk that the movie industry is riddled with reds. Yet the highest estimate of Communist party members in Hollywood that we could find was 200 at any one time. Those who used the movies as a whipping boy for their prejudices were smearing tens of thousands of non-Communists. This sort of thing cannot happen if we insist upon authoritative evidence to back up all charges of Communist infiltration.

4. Rejecting smears of non-Communists. Every such smear adds to the strength of the party. It serves to identify communism with worthy measures and good men. It tends to keep people in the party through fear of being smeared if they leave. Communists themselves have developed the smear to a high level of efficiency. But their own smears often depend for their success upon the readiness of the unwary to accept unsubstantiated charges.

5. Above all, remember that the world is an exciting, nonstatic organism and that people change their minds as the world forces shift and that the cruelest of all behavior patterns consist in the use of attainder—the process of non-correction, nonredemption, and perpetual damnation. Obviously this whole program is predicated on the theory that it is more desirable to salvage than to smash a Communist. The rehabilitation of enough Communists will deprive the party of its main source of strength. The smashing of the individual member or former member

destroys a lot of people but can never damage an underground party.

Finally, and most important of all, is the need for a steady, persistent campaign on behalf of our positive beliefs. Free men quite properly have little use for those who are chronically "agin" something. Progress is made not merely by opposing an evil program but by working and, if necessary, fighting for a good one. Therefore, the best insurance against communism—or any other undesirable *ism*—is a constructive campaign to strengthen the freedoms and opportunities we now enjoy. The basis of any such campaign is education. To be successful, education must be affirmative. We may profitably explain other ideas so that our reasons for opposing them are understood. But that is not enough unless our own ideas and ideals are expounded with conviction and understanding. This is so basic a tenet in the educational process that it may be taken for granted. It must not be taken too much for granted.

The individuals who have contributed to this book were well worth salvaging. We doubt that they are appreciably different in this respect from present party members— many of whom are thinking about how to get out. But even if we did not think so, we would advocate the same program. In a war one does not ask a deserter from the enemy if he is sure he repents sincerely and completely his term of service with the foe. We are glad to get a reduction in the strength of the opposing army. Yet present attitudes toward the former Communist are much harsher than toward an enemy deserter. One of the most objective of the former Communists we interviewed, one who seemed happier than most, as well as less bitter, told us he thought it was too bad that Communists were kept in the party because they were afraid "a Senator or Congressman needed a headline more than our nation needed a convert from communism to democracy." He added thoughtfully:

"It would not take much to start a stampede of present Communists under 25 years of age to the offices of the FBI. All it needs is that the Committees of Congress act as if they really wanted men and women to get out of the party."

We only wish to add that this also should be the attitude of our whole society, not just the responsibility of members of Congress.

CAPRICORN GIANTS

204. *Brockelmann*, ISLAMIC PEOPLES. $1.95.
205. *Salter*, CONDITIONED REFLEX THERAPY. $1.75.
206. *Lissner*, LIVING PAST. $1.95.
207. *Davis*, CORPORATIONS. $2.45.
208. *Rodman*, CONVERSATION WITH ARTISTS. $1.45.
209. *Falls*, GREAT WAR 1914-1918. $1.95.
210. MEMOIRS OF A RENAISSANCE POPE. $1.85.
211. *Schachner*, FOUNDING FATHERS, $2.45.
212. *Viereck*, THE UNADJUSTED MAN. $1.85.
213. *Cournos, ed.*, ANTHOLOGY OF CLASSIC RUSSIAN LITERA-TURE. $2.45.
215. *Guerdan*, BYZANTIUM. $1.45.
216. *Mandeville*, THE FABLE OF THE BEES. $1.65.
217. *Bradford*, OF PLYMOUTH PLANTATION. $1.65.
218. *Taylor*, THE COURSE OF GERMAN HISTORY. $1.45.
219. *Frankfurter*, LAW AND POLITICS. $1.65.
220. *Little*, GEORGE WASHINGTON. $1.95.
221. *Peterson*, ANCIENT MEXICO. $1.65.
223. *Isaacs*, AMERICA AND THE ORIENT. $1.85.
224. *Hartwich*, ABERRATIONS OF SEXUAL LIFE. $1.95.
225. *Frank*, LAW AND THE MODERN MIND. $1.65.
226. *Grekov*, SOVIET CHESS. $1.65.
227. *Ernst & Loth*, REPORT ON THE AMERICAN COMMUNIST. $1.45.

G. P. PUTNAM'S SONS

200 Madison Avenue ● New York 16, N. Y.